CREATED to WORSHIP

A Practical Guide
to Leading the
Christian Assembly

Created to
WORSHIP

Ken E. Read

College Press Publishing Company • Joplin, Missouri

Library of Congress Cataloging-in-Publication Data

Read, Ken (Kenneth Eugene), 1957–
    Created to worship: a practical guide to leading the Christian
assembly / Ken Read
        p.   cm.
    ISBN 0-89900-907-7
    1. Public Worship   I. Title
BV15.R42 2002
264—dc21   2002067581

TABLE ·OF· CONTENTS

PART 1: FINDING WHERE WE ARE

PART 2: DISCOVERING WHERE WE WANT TO BE

PART 3: DETERMINING HOW TO GET THERE

PART 4: LEADING IN THE JOURNEY

FOREWORD

The subject of worship has become popular over the course of the past two decades. No other period of Church history has witnessed such an interest as in this modern period. Go to any Christian bookstore and you will find a healthy stock of worship recordings and books. In light of this surge of material, it is legitimate to ask if the Church needs yet another book on worship.

My response is a resounding, "Yes!" Dr. Ken Read has insightfully put together a work that should cause serious-minded Church leaders to ponder important issues. Dr. Read is especially gifted at raising questions that need to be raised. He thoughtfully examines both the heart and the practice of praise and worship in today's Church.

Although his emphasis is upon the practical issues related to worship in our corporate gatherings, Dr. Read carefully and insightfully factors in the true foundation of "why we do what we do." That one and only foundation is a solid focus upon God–His greatness, His glory, and His marvelous qualities. It is precisely this backdrop that brings meaning to a relevant discussion of practical matters.

The golden thread that runs throughout this entire work is the notion of our destiny and purpose as followers of Jesus. We have been created for worship. This incredible truth has temporal and eternal bearing upon all that we are, all that we do, and all that we possess. Our gifts and talents, on every level, become exceedingly significant in light of this great revelation. Our sense of fulfillment and our sense of meaning rest entirely on this foundation. Our hearts, out of which flow the issues of life itself, are at stake in light of the choices we make during our brief sojourn upon this earth. All this is directly related to the all-important issue of worship.

The truth is undeniable: everyone worships. Every person ever born gives devotion and adoration to someone or something. Only we can determine the object of that devotion. Ken Read holds before us, as individuals and churches, the Great Objective of all time, the majestic and loving Lord of the Universe Himself.

If you are part of a church that is traditional or progressive, blended or contemporary, you will find this work both thought provoking and well worth your investment of time. Dr. Read is an expert at turning over every stone. He is not afraid to tangle with tough and uncomfortable issues. Use this book in your small group as a stimulus to study and discussion. Above all, allow this present work to cause you to worship Him, Whose greatness no one can fully fathom!

John G. Elliott
Songwriter, recording artist,
and worship leader

PREFACE

THANKSGIVING

This book grows out of more than a decade of teaching Worship Leadership and other courses at Cincinnati Bible College and Seminary. I am forever grateful to the administration of the school for allowing me the freedom to shape the courses as I saw fit, and for the confidence shown in the material to allow me to teach them year after year. Teaching these courses, revisiting and revising the material virtually every semester, has helped me in leading worship in my own local church immensely. I am also grateful to the students, many of whom have hungered for authentic worship to the point that they have spurred me on to finding answers to their questions. Students have more than once driven me to study, to passion, and to reflection for the topic of worship in the church.

The material also is derived from the several worship consultations and worship seminars done in local churches over the years. I appreciate those who have asked the hard questions and taught me about "real life" in their churches. Sometimes answers that seem so easy on paper or in the classroom are not so simple when tried with flesh-and-blood people.

I have served six churches to date as some sort of professional worship leader, over a time period of more than 25 years. Senior ministers and mentors have helped me immensely to learn some lessons about who God is and how His people work. So, thanks to Jerry, Lee, Willard, Pat, Mike, and Dan for your encouragement and patience while I experimented and you watched.

THE RESTORATION MOVEMENT

This book has been developed through my experience as a worship leader within the Restoration Movement, sometimes known as the Stone/Campbell Movement. Most Christians from other backgrounds will find the material here to be helpful in their situations as well, but from time to time this book will address the problems and blessings that come directly from the heritage of independent Christian churches and instrumental churches of Christ.

For those readers who are not familiar with that heritage, this introduction may provide some needed background: The Restoration Movement was begun in America in the early 1800s, and was articulated by men such as Alexander Campbell and Barton W. Stone. The plea was to become Christians simply, with no further denominational or sectarian identification or loyalties. Slogans such as "No creed but Christ, no book but the Bible" or "In essentials unity, in opinions liberty, in all things charity" or "Not the only Christians, but Christians only" helped to voice the commonality of these churches. The movement came to be known as the Restoration Movement (seeking to restore the New Testament church in its polity, practices, and fruit), and it grew quickly in the 1800s, especially on the frontier of what we now know as Middle America.

In the years since, some of the congregations' reorganized into (ironically) a denomination, which eventually associated with the ecumenical movement of the late twentieth century. This branch has come to be known as the Disciples of Christ, with the name Christian Church over their doors. Other congregations[2] were more radically conservative and were opposed to the use of mechanical musical instruments; these churches came to prefer the moniker "church of Christ."

The churches with which I have primarily been associated are of a centrist group within this Restoration Movement, sometimes called Christian churches (independent—so as to say not Disciples of Christ) or churches of Christ (instrumental—so as to indicate that they are not noninstrumental). The churches have no denominational organization or headquarters although they mutually cooperate in supporting mission work (International Disaster relief, campus ministries, and many missionaries), publishing enterprises (Standard Publishing, College Press, and a directory of the ministry, for example), and education (Bible colleges and Christian service camps). The churches tend to be theologically conservative, pragmatic in methodology, and broadly evangelical. They might be distinguished from other evangelical groups in that they baptize by immersion for the forgiveness of sin, and they celebrate the Lord's Supper every week. They tend to be rural and suburban and predominantly white American middle class, though many are changing this image.

Introduction

Why Another Book on Worship?

There are books being written on the subject of worship all the time. Worship books talk about theology, history, prayer, or perhaps an overview of worship or a pep talk on personal worship. I read and enjoy them all with enthusiasm, and none is without merit. However, I rarely find a *practical* book on worship leading from a perspective that matches most of the churches with which I work. There are several practical books on worship leading from a praise-and-worship perspective, and some practical books on more formal worship leading. There are few that cover the whole spectrum of what worship traditions might be covered in churches of evangelicalism, much less of the Restoration Movement.

Because of this dearth, I have gradually developed my own material, which was compiled into a syllabus. That syllabus has slowly grown into a book. And now, it will be available to those churches that seem to need this kind of book.

What Do You Mean by "Worship?"

The word, "worship" is used in so many ways, it seems to have every meaning possible. It is a noun ("the worship," synonymous to assembly, gathering, service, or liturgy), it is a verb ("I worship," similar to adore, serve, bow down, or revere), and it is a modifier (a worship song, worship concert, or worship pastor). It seems the meaning is so diverse, that it is hard to pin down what we mean by it when we talk about it. "Worship" means everything, and consequently can mean nothing. Throughout this book, I am aware of the struggle. So recognize that for the most part I try to be consistent in using the word "assembly" when referring to the "worship service." And when I talk about "worship leadership," I am speaking of the act of leading others in the activities and expressions within that assembly.

How to Use This Book

Primarily the book is targeted for group study, to be done by a group of those who are largely responsible for the worship leading in a local church: the musicians, the elders, the staff, perhaps the servers and certainly those who do the planning. It is also designed to be a textbook for college classes for those who will work with developing worship in a church body as well as those who will themselves be worship leaders. Many of the activities are designed for group discussion and interaction. The book could be used by an individual, certainly; but the material is best absorbed if it is discussed with another person.

PART ONE

Finding Where We Are

CHAPTER ONE

Introducing Ourselves

What is your worship experience background?

My Stories

W e all come from some set of preconceptions and biases. I need to tell you mine by telling you three stories about me. Then I will give you a chance to tell your stories and provide some exercises to help you assess your church.

Understand this first of all: I did not grow up as a Christian from birth, so I did not grow up with a love for churches and their traditions. I was baptized in my early teens and took off spiritually during my high school years. That was back in the days when we would sit in a circle in our bell-bottomed jeans and 35 of us with 6 guitars would sing all of the choruses that were our "own." Yes, sir. That was *real* worship; and it will probably never be the same again.

So I grew up with a different set of traditions. I remember, as a cynical idealistic teenager, sitting in church as we dragged through one hymn after another. Services seemed to plow thoughtlessly through the same slow succession of organ prelude to silent roll call cards to prayer hymn to prayer time to communion hymn to meditations and serving rituals. I thought, *Do they actually think this is full of life? Does anybody get anything out of this week after week? Or do they not care? Maybe that's it; maybe they are all so spiritually insensitive they don't even notice that no one is coming, no one is touched, no one is changed.* I came to the wrong conclusion. They weren't spiritually dead, any more than I was spiritually mature.

These days neither "their" system nor "my" style of worship will "work" anymore. God never changes; culture always does. So, my brethren and I both find ourselves asking the same questions again:

(?) "How can we make our assemblies vital, life-changing, and relevant, without being offensive?"

(?) "How can we reach people for Christ, while at the same time equipping the saints for service, while at the same time worshiping the Lord Almighty acceptably?"

(?) "What kind of music and worship style will communicate authentically to this generation?"

That's my first story. The second is this: I have always considered myself to be something of a stoic and an intellectual. I would have wanted my friends to describe me as reserved, controlled, and intelligent. So when I became a Christian, I was more or less converted to the Christian philosophy. I was a firm believer from the neck up. My spiritual growth was measured by Scripture memorized, by truths learned, and by disciplines mastered.

My senior year in college I roomed with a new convert who was charismatic. I thought it a happy opportunity for this young neophyte to be able to spend time with me, that I might help to bring balance and wisdom to his young, emotionally-driven faith. What I didn't see was how out of balance I was myself.

One day, for some reason, I allowed the walls to come down and make myself vulnerable, and I actually confided in Ron. "You know, we all talk about a personal relationship with Christ. I don't think I'm missing anything, but yet I'm not sure that I could say I know Christ personally. What do you think?"

Ron said, "Ken, do you ever adore God? When you are in your prayer closet, how much time do you spend worshiping Him?"

Up to that time I had not given thought to the concept of personal worship. I knew *about* God, but I had not let myself dwell on Him, His character or His attributes. I said the words of worship in public, but I had not spent private time seeking His face or giving myself to the experiential side of spiritual communion with the God of the Universe.

Ron's words sent me on a journey that I still travel with joy. I can now say that my greatest goal is to know Christ. Through worship we experience the practice of a personal relationship with Christ. To some degree this book is a chronicle of that pilgrimage.

My third story is from an unpleasant experience I share with many of my friends in music ministry. I came to a church, having been given the stated goal of taking them to more "contemporary" worship (whatever that means!). But when we started using music that was culturally relevant for the target group we had identified, I found myself under severe criticism from church members.

In fact, I found that I had become the lightning rod of criticism for every discontent in the church. If I used traditional music, the young people lost interest and left for a more "hip" church. If I did contemporary music, the old people complained. If I achieved a careful balance, blending both traditional and contemporary, I was shot at from both sides. I learned the hard way that people do not just **have** opinions about music; they **feel** opinions about music. They may not be able to articulate what they like, but they sure can speak clearly about what they **don't** like.

And so this book is for my wounded friends in music ministry. My great hope is that every church will find a positive vision for what worship can be. May our assemblies be unifying, and may we find healing and power in celebrating the Lord and sharing His gospel.

THE HIGHEST PRIORITY

What is the meaning of life? **Reason** tells us that worship is the key to understanding why we are here. I was a teenager, cutting my grandmother's grass one day, and I wondered as I wandered about the meaning of life. I thought, *Some people act as if the only meaning is "Me." Get what I can, because soon I'll be gone, and who knows what then?* Then, I thought, *Other people say the meaning of life is to help others, not to live for self.* "We" sounds more noble than "Me," but in truth, it only expands the circle to include other mortals like myself.

So, if "Me" and "We" is not the meaning of life, what is? A look at the universe should tell us that "He" is the meaning of life. **Nature** agrees with reason that we are here to glorify God and to fit into the whole universe that sings the song of the symphony of praise.

You ask, "Why worship?" You may as well ask, "Why does a fish swim, why does a bird fly, why does a tree bring forth leaves, why does a river flow downstream?" The answer is the same for all: that's what they were created to do, and in doing those things they glorify their Maker. So God created us in His image that we might give Him the highest praise. The sun, the moon, the stars, the clouds, the rain, the blue; it all says there's a God, and He is not you! It tells of mercy and renewal, of faithfulness and beauty, of majesty and strength.

Scripture also tells us of the importance of worship. From the first words of Genesis, when God created all there was; when, according to Job, the morning stars sang together, the glory of God has been the theme of their song. The psalmist reiterates the theme when he says the heavens are telling the glory of God and the earth proclaims His handiwork.

The glory of God can also be seen in the New Testament book of Romans, where it says that since the creation of the world God's invisible qualities (His eternal power and divine nature) have been clearly seen, being understood from what has been made. Then concluding with the great "Alleluias" and "Worthy is the Lamb" and the "new songs" in the book of Revelation, we see that the theme of all creation, indeed of all of history, has been *worship*. If Redemption is the scarlet thread running throughout the tapestry of Scripture, worship is the golden loom on which it was woven.

Worship is the most important thing for us to grasp. Until my senior year of college, I missed out on—and I don't want you to miss out on—a personal relationship of adoration with God. Worship involves more than knowing *about* God, but knowing God Himself. Worship is the greatest theme of the Bible; the ultimate priority, the eternal dividing line, the *sine qua non*, the central focus, the ultimate superlative. Worship is why we are here on earth.

The Westminster catechism begins with this question: "What is the chief end of man?" Depending on our background, we might tend to think that the answer would be, "The chief end of man is to be righteous," or "The chief end of man is to win the lost." But those are not the answer in the catechism. The answer is, "The chief end of man is to glorify God and to enjoy Him forever." Worship is the chief end of man. And worship is to be fun!

You and I were born to worship the Lord. If worship is so important, then what is worship? In this book I will not give a definition, for Scripture doesn't define it. But, I'd like to recommend that it is four different things as we explore it together.

Recognize Who God Is

First of all, worship is recognizing **who God is**. Worship of God, acceptable worship in His sight, must include recognition of the nature of the One worshiped. Who is He? He is holy. He is the Being One. He is eternal. He is different from all man-made gods.

When we take a good, long look at the nature of God, it begins to transform our own character. We tend to become like the one whom we worship, whether a sports hero, a human concept, or an eternal, all-powerful God. As a matter of fact, God wants it that way. God Himself said, "Be holy, as I the Lord am holy." Jesus added, "Be perfect, even as your Father who is in heaven is perfect." John wrote,

"Dear friends, since God so loved us, so we ought to love one another." Suddenly, worship becomes practical! True worship actually is the best means of self-improvement, rather than religious works and New Year's resolutions. We focus on our goal, Jesus, the author and finisher of our faith, and He changes us from the inside out.

Praise God for What He Does

Worship is also praising God for **what He has done**. Humble adoration is our response to discovering who God *is*, but thankful praise has to do with what He *does*. We praise a child for a drawing that he or she has made. We praise an employee for a job well done. So we praise God for His works.

Ephesians 5:19-20 says we are to **"speak to one another with songs, hymns and spiritual songs. Sing and make melody in your hearts to the Lord, always giving thanks to God the Father for everything, in the name of our Lord Jesus Christ."**

Why did the Father bother with us in the first place? If He knew we were going to fall, that Adam and Eve were just going to sin, that there would be all this hassle with the flood and sin and wickedness, why did He create us in His image with a free will and an ability to fall? Why did He do it? It is so that we would worship Him! We appreciate love much more when the person gives it with a free will. When we could walk away and we choose to stay, the worship is so much grander.

The most popular praise chorus in the Old Testament is, "His mercy endureth forever," or "His lovingkindness is everlasting," or "His love endures forever," depending on the translation. Do you know why Israel sang that refrain so often? Because they had to rely on the Lord's mercy so much! Their very history underscores the fact that God's mercy endures forever. Their sinfulness was almost as long as His mercy. Consider times when God came close to wiping out mankind in the Flood, or Israel in the wilderness. Consider Israel's history as recorded in the book of Judges, as over and over they went through the cycle of oppression, repentance, deliverance, backsliding, and bondage again.

But do you know what? The song about the Lord's love is the song for all of us as well. Our sinfulness lasts a long time. That's true. But God's mercy endures forever. Ephesians 2 has some significant verses that might escape us if we read through them too quickly. Paul has reminded the believers that they had been dead in sin and had been made alive in Christ. In verses 4-6, he writes,

> But because of his great love for us, God, who is rich in mercy, made us alive with Christ even when we were dead in transgressions—it is by grace you have been saved. And God raised us up with Christ and seated us with him in the heavenly realms in Christ Jesus, in order that in the coming ages he might show the incomparable riches of his grace, expressed in his kindness to us in Christ Jesus.

Take a look at it again. Why did He save us? Why did He raise us up? Why did He make what was dead alive? Why does He set us in the heavenly places in Christ Jesus? He does all that so that He can show the riches of His grace to us. John MacArthur says that we are, in a sense, God's trophy case for all of eternity. When the angels come to Him and say, "God, how loving are You?" He'll turn and point to you and me and say, "Do you see how loving I am? See this one! I've forgiven every sin and in Christ Jesus I have allowed this one into My presence." Because of God and His great mercy we are able to worship and praise and give thanks.

PRESENT YOURSELF BACK TO GOD

A third aspect of worship is to actively respond to His nature and His deeds, by **presenting ourselves back** to God. Romans 12 urges us, after taking a good, long look at the mercies of God and the forgiveness that He has given us, to turn the gift around and give ourselves back to Him as living sacrifices, which is our spiritual act of worship.

Oftentimes we get the drama of worship backwards. Kierkegaard was the first to explain it: We sometimes mistakenly think of the preacher, worship leader, or other up-front people as being the performers, the congregation as the audience, and God as sort of a prompter in the wings helping ensure that the "show" goes well. But that model is wrong. In the drama of worship, God Himself is the audience, the congregation (I am careful never to call them the audience) is the performer for Him. The up-front people (including the worship leader) are merely the prompters, providing material so that the congregation can offer up a better performance for that audience of One.

Worship, of course, is far more than just a Sunday morning experience. Many people come to worship on Sunday morning (of course not Sunday evening; they have busy schedules), and they think they're all right with God because they've given God their hour or two per week. But if we are called to be a living sacrifice, then that means God wants control of every detail of our lives, not just one. Every detail? **"Whether you eat or drink, or whatever you do, do it for the glory of God"** (1 Cor. 10:31). When we review God's mercies, our response is to give ourselves as a sacrifice in return.

CORPORATE CREATIVE CELEBRATION

Lastly, corporate worship is also **creative celebration**. Private worship is all day every day, but in the corporate assembly worship takes on a special significance. There is something special about the body of Christ coming together to demonstrate the unity that we have in Christ, to encourage one another, and to build one another up. Hebrews 10:24-25 says that we are not to neglect the gathering of ourselves together, as is the habit of some, but we are to *encourage one another*, and all the more as we see the Day approaching. We come for the Lord, and we come for one another.

Worship need not be some stuffy ritual done solely out of duty, although it is a command. Worship can be alive, often spontaneous, sometimes public and perhaps untraditional. It can be done by singing unto the Lord, dancing before Him, rejoicing in His presence, lifting hands unto Him, or offering Him works of fine art. In short, God made us in His image, and part of that image is being creative. The God who created all that there is, is honored and worshiped when we demonstrate His likeness by our own creativity.

One of the greatest evangelistic tools for the church is exciting, creative worship. It is a false choice to think that we have to choose worship *or* evangelism. When true worship happens in the assembly, God uses us to draw people to Himself. When a revival occurs in a church, the lively activity attracts those who need life. But, as Jesus said in Luke 17, where there is a dead body there the vultures will gather. The greatest evangelistic tool is a changed life, and worship involves life change.

Worship: The Highest Calling

God's priorities for us may surprise us a bit, depending on our church backgrounds. Some of us grew up thinking that God was primarily interested in *our behavior*; that if we did the right things, the Lord would be pleased (or at least would be less angry). Some of us were taught that God was primarily interested in having us *share the gospel* and that His first goal was to save the world. Still others of us grew up thinking that God's first priority was to *give us an abundant life*; that He who loves us so much wants to bless us. All of these are important to the Lord. But let me suggest that worship is His highest, greatest, and first priority for our lives.

"Worship Moments"

Occasionally in our lives we have defining moments, which affect us profoundly. In these moments, we see God in a new way, and our relationship with Him is changed forever. For lack of a better term, let's call these personal glimpses of the eternal "worship moments."

A Memorable Moment!

The apostle John had such a worship moment, which he records in Revelation chapter 1. He writes, "**On the Lord's Day I was in the Spirit.**" He was worshiping privately already on the first day of the week, and it became an experience that he remembered afterward. Remember where you were when certain life-changing events happened? The very place and day are marked in our memories for life. Worship moments like these are common in Scripture, and seem to follow a similar pattern as John's Revelation experience. Isaiah saw the Lord in the year King Uzziah died (Isaiah 6); Saul, who became Paul, was on the road to Damascus (Acts 9, 22, 26); Peter was fasting and praying on the rooftop of Simon (Acts 10). Where were you when God broke through?

SEEING THE LORD: GLORY!

On that memorable day, the Lord Jesus Christ intervened with a vision of Himself in His glory. John says,

> I heard behind me a loud voice like a trumpet. . . . I turned around to see the voice that was speaking to me. And when I turned I saw . . . someone "like a son of man," dressed in a robe reaching down to his feet and with a golden sash around his chest. His head and hair were white like wool, as white as snow, and his eyes were like blazing fire. His feet were like bronze glowing in a furnace, and his voice was like the sound of rushing waters. In his right hand he held seven stars, and out of his mouth came a sharp double-edged sword. His face was like the sun shining in all its brilliance (Revelation 1:10,12-16).

Similarly, Isaiah saw the Lord high and lifted up in the Temple; Paul saw a blinding light; Peter had a vision of a conversation with Jesus about unclean animals. Perhaps our worship moments are not as dramatic as a vision from God, but occasionally we do have those rare moments when we see Him in a new light, and it leaves a permanent mark in our memories.

OUR RESPONSE: FEAR!

John's response was common for those who see the Lord for all that He is: "When I saw him, I fell at his feet as though dead." Likewise, after seeing a miraculous catch of fish, Peter said, "Depart from me, for I am a sinful man, O Lord" (Luke 5:8). Isaiah cried out, "Woe to me! . . . I am ruined! For I am a man of unclean lips, and I live among a people of unclean lips, and my eyes have seen the

King, the LORD **Almighty**" (Isa. 6:5). The shepherds outside of Bethlehem were terrified (Luke 2). Fear and awe are human responses to the majesty and other-ness of God.

God's Action: Comfort!

But God's first action when meeting people is to assure us not to be afraid: "**Then he placed his right hand on me and said: 'Do not be afraid. I am the First and the Last. I am the Living One; I was dead, and behold I am alive for ever and ever! And I hold the keys of death and Hades.**" The Lord or His messenger spoke similar words to Isaiah, to Paul, to Moses (Exodus 3), to the shepherds, to the disciples after the resurrection (John 20), and to others. God lets us see His glory, then assures us of His love.

God's Call: Commission!

Once the Lord has us where we need to be, seeing Him, being awed and reassured, He is ready to commission us to do His will. In John's case, Jesus said, "**Write, therefore, what you have seen, what is now and what will take place later.**" He similarly invited Isaiah, Paul, Peter, the shepherds, the disciples, and others to go and do His bidding. And after what they had experienced, His people did it willingly.

So, what about you? Have you had a defining moment, when your life was changed by an encounter with the living and awesome, eternal God? I have had a few. Like the time I was reading 1 Corinthians 8:1 and I was suddenly turned around by the realization of how spiritually proud I was while I pursued learning rather than learning how to love. Or the time that I was reflecting during the Lord's Supper one Sunday. I imagined how big the universe is, and then how small the particles of an atom are. Then I realized that the God of both the macrocosm and the microcosm knows me intimately and loves me, and that Jesus died for me personally.

Let me ask you to tell about a "worship moment" for you (however you would describe a "worship moment"). This is a very personal question, but it could help us understand worship leadership much better if we first understand when we have been changed by worship. Describe briefly what happened when you were allowed a glimpse of the eternal. Perhaps it was at a concert, or at camp, or when you were walking through the woods. Perhaps it was at a crusade, in a small group, or in private prayer. Some examples from students are included here.

"I was really struggling with the temptations of sin and was feeling overwhelmed. I knew I just couldn't take much more. I was studying in a personal Bible study and came across a scripture I had never heard nor read previously. I Corinthians 10:13. God will not let you be tempted beyond what you can bear. This really hit home. I realized I could overcome the temptation. ***I immediately gave thanks to God*** and asked for His help."

"My most memorable worship moment came at my first CIY conference in Adrian, Michigan. We were in a main session singing before the message. ***I felt the presence of the Lord at that time more than I ever had before.*** There was something about thousands of teenagers singing and worshiping along with me that made it very special. We all seemed to be in tune with the songs and their message. It was a great experience and one I won't forget."

"It was a trip with the youth group to Gatlinburg, Tennessee. We had been singing and worshiping outside until it started to rain. We headed back inside and continued. ***The worship lasted around three hours and during the time we could see God at work outside but also feel His presence inside.***"

"One of my memorable worship moments happened during the spring semester of 1995. I traveled with a group from school during Urban Ministry Weekend to Charleston, West Virginia. That Sunday we attended a black inner-city church, which is something that I had not experienced before. It was a remarkable experience because they worshiped in such a lively way. To put it in their words, they had the Spirit. ***They clapped, they prayed and they sang with their whole hearts.*** This experience was very encouraging to me because it helped me to better understand that people worship in their own ways. It also helped me to better understand that there is freedom in worship and we need to honor that freedom by allowing it."

"I was in a public worship assembly. A young lady was singing a solo and the sound system went crazy with weird sounds. It certainly took everyone out of their comfort zone. The sound people quickly fixed the sound, she sang the song again and ***God came in power and presence. It was a continually impromptu time of personal praise and singing to the Lord for over an hour.***"

Now, for some reflection on this project:

What are some of the common factors for these worship moments?

- ➡ Most of them happen at times other than Sunday morning.
- ➡ They are usually taking place in a setting in which someone was initially out of their comfort zone.
- ➡ They usually involve creativity.
- ➡ They are almost always unexpected surprises, and are very personal.
- ➡ They seldom involve a person being manipulated.
- ➡ Often they involve music, and people are emotionally engaged.
- ➡ Other:

_____

_____

_____

_____

This is what we want to have happen in our churches!

Reflection/Application:

Introducing Ourselves

Now, let's find out about you, about your home church and/or the church where you attend and serve now. How would you describe the worship in your church, using the scales or spectra below?

Traditional   1   2   3   4   5   6   7   **Contemporary**

Describe the instrumentation and style of music (a cappella ... organ and piano ... orchestra ... praise band with drums ... gospel quartet, etc.)

_____

Length of service (60 min.......120 min......180 min.) _____

Preaching style (expository ... revivalistic ... informal ... relational ... thematic ... seeker ... topical series, etc.)

_____

Subjective/emotional 1   2   3   4   5   6   7   **Objective/rational**

Reverent/formal   1   2   3   4   5   6   7   **Casual/informal**

Now, rate your Sunday morning service from 1-10. If you give the worship assembly a rating of 10, that means every week it is life-changing and always sends you away closer in your walk with the Lord. If you give it a 1, that means it never seems to "work" for anyone, as far as you can see. It is the worst hour of your week, which you barely endure, simply because you love God and go out of obedience to Him and love for His people.

Your rating of Sunday morning: _____

How about Sunday night? What would your rating be for that service? _____

Do you have Wednesday night worship? Many churches are using Wednesday nights for contemporary celebration services, which include a more extensive time of worship and praise than Sunday morning has.

If your church has such a service, how do you rate it? _____

Do you have "worship time" in small groups in your church? Again, provide a rating for how that worship seems to "work": _____

What do you conclude about worship in your church, based on your answers so far?

Worship Moments:

Tell about a worship moment for you:

CHAPTER TWO
ASSESSING MY CHURCH

IDENTIFYING OUR TRADITIONS.

A DO-IT-YOURSELF WORSHIP CONSULTATION

On occasion I do "worship consultations" with congregations. This chapter contains the material that I use and what I do in those consultations. It is designed for you to do your own worship consultation, as if you were an outsider observing your assembly for the first time. With this method, you can make some observations, draw some conclusions, and give some recommendations. Are you ready to put on your analyst's hat? Here we go.

We are going to assess your church in five steps. The goal is first to identify our values as a congregation. Remember, assessment is first a nonjudgmental measurement of "where we are," not a weapon for arguing over "where we need to be." There are, no doubt, as many different opinions about your worship assembly as there are people attending it, so trying to get a big enough picture without personal bias is always a challenge. So the first objective here is to delay judgment and affirm the apparent values of the body as they stand. After that, the leadership can determine what values and direction they want for the future. Let this chapter serve as a catalyst for healthy discussion in your church.

Step One: How Do We Spend Our Time? Budgeting Time in the Assembly

The first step is to discreetly videotape one of your church's assemblies, in order to assess your congregation's worship values in actual practice. We may say that certain aspects of worship are very important to us, but our actual use of time may betray our true values. So, we start with this objective view, in order to measure what we actually **do**, not just what we **think** we do or what we **want** to do.

Some practical advice: Bring an outsider into your assembly, someone whose opinions you trust. In addition, you can discreetly videotape one or two of your church services and view them as an outsider yourself. Then have a group join you to watch the videotape objectively, with stopwatch in hand. Make note of the time at every change of events and decide how to categorize it (sometimes that is difficult to determine). Then, assess what you see. Categorize the time similar to this:

TIME REPORT		
Clock Time:	**Elapsed Time:**	**Event or Activity:** (Describe or categorize)
10:23:07	08:38	Prelude
10:31:45	00:33	Welcome and Prayer
10:32:18	00:14	Organ introduction
10:32:32	03:33	Congregational singing (hymn)
10:36:05	00:06	Silence
10:36:11	__:__	XXXXXXXXXXXXXXXXX
__:__:__	XX:XX	XXXXXXXXXXXXXXXX
XX:XX:XX	XX:XX	XXXXXXXXXXXXXXXX
XX:XX:XX	XX:XX	XXXXXXXXXXXXXXXX

Figure 2.1 Time Report Chart

TIME REPORT

Clock Time: Elapsed Time: Event or Activity: (Describe or categorize)

___:___:___   ___:___

___:___:___   ___:___

___:___:___   ___:___

___:___:___   ___:___

___:___:___   ___:___

___:___:___   ___:___

___:___:___   ___:___

___:___:___   ___:___

___:___:___   ___:___

___:___:___   ___:___

___:___:___   ___:___

___:___:___   ___:___

___:___:___   ___:___

___:___:___   ___:___

___:___:___   ___:___

___:___:___   ___:___

___:___:___   ___:___

___:___:___   ___:___

___:___:___   ___:___

___:___:___   ___:___

___:___:___   ___:___

___:___:___   ___:___

___:___:___   ___:___

___:___:___   ___:___

___:___:___   ___:___

___:___:___   ___:___

___:___:___   ___:___

___:___:___   ___:___

___:___:___   ___:___

___:___:___   ___:___

___:___:___   ___:___

___:___:___   ___:___

TIME ANALYSIS

CONGREGATIONAL SINGING

	Introduction	Singing	How well do they participate? (rank 1-10)
1. First Song	___:___	___:___	___
2. Next Song	___:___	___:___	___
3. Next Song	___:___	___:___	___
4. Next Song	___:___	___:___	___
5. Next Song	___:___	___:___	___
6. Next Song	___:___	___:___	___
7. Next Song	___:___	___:___	___
8. Next Song	___:___	___:___	___
9. Next Song	___:___	___:___	___
10. Next Song	___:___	___:___	___
11.			Total elapsed time CS: ___:___

OTHER CONGREGATIONAL PARTICIPATION

What kind?	How many?	Elapsed time	How well? (1-10)
12. Responses	___	___:___	___
13. Individual testimonies or sharing	___	___:___	___
14. Prayer requests	___	___:___	___
15. Greeting and sharing time	___	___:___	___
16. Ministry time at response	___	___:___	___
17. Other: _____	___	___:___	___
18.			Total elapsed time CP: ___:___

MUSICAL PRESENTATION

What kind?	How many?	Elapsed time
19. Vocal solos	___	___:___
20. Instrumental music	___	___:___
21. Other: _____	___	___:___
22.		Total elapsed time MP: ___:___

PREPARED SPEAKING

What kind?	How many?	Elapsed time
23. Meditations	___	___:___
24. Transitions, worship focus, etc.	___	___:___
25. Announcements	___	___:___
26. Message/sermon	___	___:___
27. Scripture reading	___	___:___
28. Other: _____	___	___:___
29.		Total elapsed time PS: ___:___

PRAYER

What kind?	How many?	Elapsed time
30. Opening prayer	___	___:___
31. Pastoral prayer	___	___:___
32. Communion prayer	___	___:___
33. Offering prayer	___	___:___
34. Prayer before sermon	___	___:___
35. Prayer before invitation	___	___:___
36. Closing prayer	___	___:___
37. Other: _____	___	___:___
38.		Total elapsed time PR: ___:___

THE LORD'S SUPPER

What event?
(parentheses = also included elsewhere)

	How many?	Elapsed time
39. (hymn)	___	___:___
40. (meditation)	___	___:___
41. (prayer)	___	___:___
42. (Scripture reading)	___	___:___
43. Disbursement	___	___:___
44.		Total elapsed time LS: ___:___

EVANGELISM

What event?	How many?	Elapsed time	Response?
45. Invitation	___	___:___	
46. Response time	___	___:___	
47. Introductions	___	___:___	
48. Preparation for baptisms	___	___:___	
49. Baptismal service	___	___:___	
50.		Total elapsed time EV: ___:___	

SCRIPTURE READING

What event?
(parentheses = also included elsewhere)

	How many?	Elapsed time
51. During sermon	___	___:___
52. Communion preparation	___	___:___
53. Other times	___	___:___
54.		Total elapsed time SR: ___:___

"DEAD" TIME

Number of occurrences

55. "Dead" time (waiting for the next thing to start) ___   Total "dead" time: ___:___

SUMMARY		Elapsed Time
56. Congregational Singing	(from line 11 above)	___:___
57. Other Congregational Participation	(from line 18 above)	___:___
58. Musical Presentation	(from line 22 above)	___:___
59. Prepared Speaking	(from line 29 above)	___:___
60. Prayer	(from line 38 above)	___:___
61. Lord's Supper	(from line 44 above)	___:___
62. Evangelism	(from line 50 above)	___:___
63. Scripture Reading	(from line 54 above)	___:___
64. Dead Time	(from line 55 above)	___:___
65.	Total time entire service	___:___

Figure 2.2 Time Analysis Chart

Now, ask yourselves some questions:

❏ How much total time would you say the congregation spent in active participation? (Consider whether to include praying, taking communion, and giving an offering. Does the congregation actively participate with the sermon?) ___:___ The remainder of the time is passive time for the congregation. How much time is passive? ___:___. How do you feel about that ratio of active to passive?

❏ How much total time in the assembly involves music? (Consider whether you include prelude, music during prayer or offering or communion, as well as musical introductions to congregational songs.) ___:___ The rest of the time does not use music. How much time is not musical? ___:___ How do you feel about the ratio of music to non-music?

❏ Who is the "target audience" at your church? _____
_____

❏ What age group is most addressed? _____

❏ Is this a service for believers or for seekers? _____
_____

❏ What surprised you in what you saw? _____
_____

❑ What was better than you expected? _____

_____

❑ What was not as good as you expected? _____

_____

❑ What does this tell you about your values as a church, as seen by a stranger looking at your video?

❑ Do you agree with these values? Are your observations consistent with what you want?

Step Two: Who Comes to Worship? Charting Our Demographic Breakdown

It is also wise to know the subculture of your congregation, your converts, and your community. Many models and styles of worship are perfectly valid, but not appropriate for a given group of people. So, while we want to avoid stereotypes of different demographic groups, at the same time we want to know what people groups we are dealing with.

There are several companies with whom you can consult for demographic breakdowns of communities. Some of them cost hundreds of dollars, and others are free. You can start on the web with the results of the U.S. census. (*Go to* www.census.gov) Those results are far more detailed than they used to be, and your search could tell you a lot.

You can also gain much insight anecdotally by taking a simple straw poll of those in your meeting. Give yourself a 30-minute time limit, so the discussion doesn't break down or become negative. Here are some good questions to ask:

About the Leadership
What age is the preacher? (He will tend to appeal to people who are ten years older or younger than himself.)
What radio station does he listen to?
On what educational level does he speak? (Based on his vocabulary, choice of illustrations, etc.)

What is the socioeconomic status of the neighborhood where he lives?

What is the size and status of his family?

What other values does he have? (Reflected in his daily schedule, recreational choices, hobbies, children's education, etc.)

What school district does he live in (or participate in)?

Record your results on a chart (see Figure 2.3). Then use the same basic questions for the congregation.

ABOUT THE CONGREGATION

What age is the median age of the congregation? (We will tend to reach people who are ten years older or younger than ourselves.)

What radio stations do the people in this room listen to? Does that reflect the tastes of the rest of the congregation?

What is the average education level of this congregation?

What is the socioeconomic status and description of the members of this church?

What is average size and status of our families?

What other values do we have (daily schedule, children's education, etc.)?

What school districts do the families in our church represent?

Then the same questions about the community in the vicinity of the church building.

ABOUT THE NEIGHBORHOOD

What age is the median age of the neighborhood? (Census information can help here.)

What are the top radio stations in our community?

What is the average education level of this community?

What is the socioeconomic status and description of the neighborhood where the church building is located? (Again, census information can help, but you may have a better nonstatistical impression of how the area is changing.)

What is average size and status of families in this area?

What other values do we have (daily schedule, children's education, etc.)?

What school districts are near our church?

Now comes the fun part: Do all of these answers match? If so, you have a correctly-targeted worship package to reach your community. Your preacher reaches people like him, and those people are the same as the people who are in the church. Congratulations!

If not, what can be done to improve the match? (NOTE: the answer is *never* to fire the preacher! There is no superman who can equally do it all. It may be, however, to openly assess where he does not match the demographics of the community and find ways to support him with staff or volunteers.) Give yourselves a few minutes to brainstorm on possible solutions.

Notice that this exercise only indirectly applies to the worship service itself. But within the first 30 seconds, any new visitor from your neighborhood has noticed and intuitively applied what has taken you as a group half an hour to decide. And within the first five minutes of your assembly, that same person has decided whether or not he or she belongs in your church, apart from whatever activities and doctrine are there. So, knowing who is out there, who is in here, and whom you tend to reach will be a significant assessment for your worship service.

Figure 2.3 Demography Chart

	Age	Education	Radio	Soc/Econ	Race	Family	Other
Preacher							
Congregation							
Community							

Models of Worship in Christian Churches

Step Three: What "Color" Is Our Worship? Picturing Our Worship Values

Thirdly, it is helpful to know what your "worship values" are, as a church. Worship values are those aspects of the assembly that your congregation and its leadership place as most important. These values will be further pursued in Step Four, in which we discuss the seven acts of public worship. This particular exercise explores your congregation's value of three basic "colors" of worship: traditional, contemporary, and thematic. Just how traditional, how contemporary, and how thematic do we want to be?

Every color can be created by a combination of three primary colors. In light (not in pigment), those colors are red, green, and blue (RGB). Just as the primary colors in combination can yield many other rich colors, so the importance placed on these three primary motivators of your worship can yield many varieties of "color" to your worship service. Each color is beautiful in itself; one is not of more value than the others. Nonetheless, once you see what color your worship is, perhaps you will decide that you would rather have a different shade. So, this exercise may be of some help in generating healthy discussion about your worship.

In the churches that I have seen, eight different basic models of worship "color" emerge. We will later explore ways to improve the service in each of these styles. **Note:** this is intended only as a *description* of styles, *not as a critique* of which ones are superior. Only one of these styles is worthy of criticism, and that is the one that has not made a choice at all.

Begin by taking this simple evaluative quiz. Chart the color of your church by answering the questions below. For each question, rate your church 0-3 according to this scale: 0=never, 1=occasionally, 2=usually, 3=always.

Figure 2.4 Color Evaluation Quiz

0=never, 1=occasionally, 2=usually, 3=always

Section 1

We sing using hymnals.	0 1 2 3
We print bulletins with an order of service.	0 1 2 3
We always offer an invitation after the sermon.	0 1 2 3
Our Communion table and pulpit remain in prominent locations on Sunday mornings.	0 1 2 3
We use piano (and organ) for congregational singing.	0 1 2 3
We take the Lord's Supper by passing trays.	0 1 2 3
We sing event-defined songs (i.e., "Prayer Hymn," Communion, invitation, and closing chorus).	0 1 2 3
Most people at our church dress more formally than they do during the week.	0 1 2 3

Section 1 Total: _____

Section 2

We sing mostly choruses.	0 1 2 3
We use guitars every week, and drums are welcomed.	0 1 2 3
Some people at our church raise their hands in worship.	0 1 2 3
We plan our singing around song sets.	0 1 2 3
Once the worship singing starts, we try not to break the flow.	0 1 2 3
We do not have a formal printed order of worship.	0 1 2 3
We project the words for singing on a wall or screen.	0 1 2 3
People tend to dress informally at church, as they would during the week.	0 1 2 3

Section 2 Total: _____

Section 3

The theme of our message is prominent (cover of bulletin, church sign, etc.).	0 1 2 3
Our worship is structured around the message of the day.	0 1 2 3
Everyone who comes to our assembly knows what the "point" was by the time they leave.	0 1 2 3
We try to explain the gospel to seekers each week.	0 1 2 3
We use drama on Sundays.	0 1 2 3
Early in each assembly, we have a spoken transition that introduces the central message.	0 1 2 3
We have a worship programming team, who puts in tremendous amounts of time planning and refining the assembly.	0 1 2 3
Our singing time is well-thought-out and organized.	0 1 2 3

Section 3 Total: _____

SUMMARY

	0-6	7-18	19-24
Section 1 Total *(blue quotient)*	_____	_____	_____
Section 2 Total *(green quotient)*	_____	_____	_____
Section 3 Total *(red quotient)*	_____	_____	_____

Figure 2.5 Worship Color Graph

Finding Your Worship "Color"

Check your Red (R), Green (G) and Blue (B) numbers from the chart above, and find the range and description here. Then read about it in the next pages.

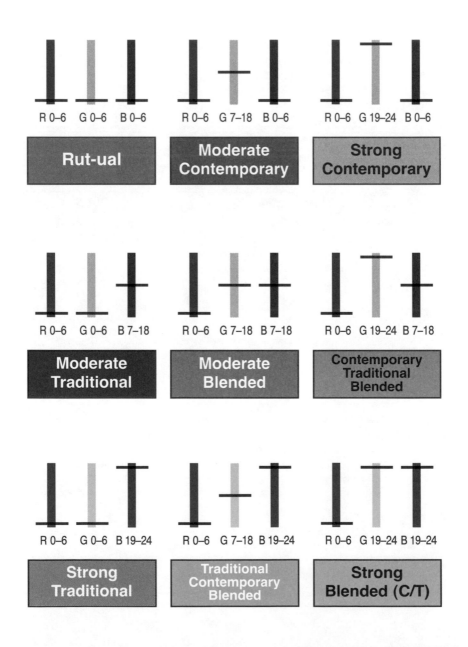

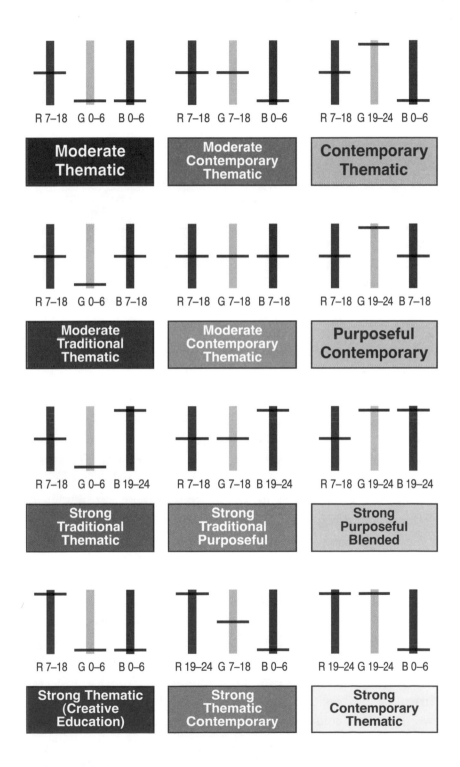

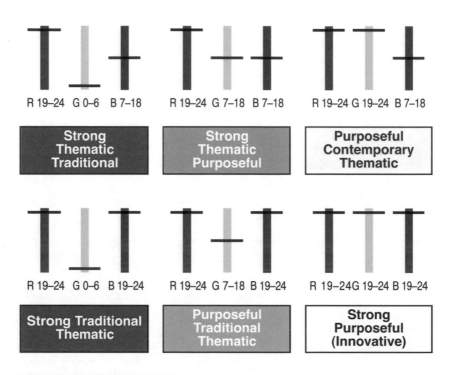

R 19–24 G 0–6 B 7–18   R 19–24 G 7–18 B 7–18   R 19–24 G 19–24 B 7–18

| Strong Thematic Traditional | Strong Thematic Purposeful | Purposeful Contemporary Thematic |

R 19–24 G 0–6 B 19–24   R 19–24 G 7–18 B 19–24   R 19–24 G 19–24 B 19–24

| Strong Traditional Thematic | Purposeful Traditional Thematic | Strong Purposeful (Innovative) |

BLUE: TRADITIONAL In Christian churches, churches that score high on the blue factor are "traditional." In the case of these evangelical churches, "traditional" style consists of an evangelistic setting with instruction. The setting springs from evangelistic crusades of the nineteenth century, consisting of a sermon with invitation, coupled with the singing of hymns and gospel songs. Sermons are central to the service and tend to be an expository or thematic series. If your church is moderate to strong in its blue scale, you probably have a semi-liturgical atmosphere, in that the service follows an order of set rituals. But the rituals take place within a "low church" setting. In Christian churches, the Lord's Supper is passed in trays, and is taken weekly. The church prints a bulletin to identify events such as "prayer hymn" or "Communion Meditation." The attire is generally rather formal (suits and ties on the men who are up front). The overall orientation is built around the *events* of the assembly; in other words, the left column of the bulletin looks almost the same week after week. Some churches have a more informal atmosphere or might have a different style of preaching, but the approach to the structure of the assembly is still considered traditional evangelical.

GREEN: CONTEMPORARY

Churches that score high on the green scale are considered contemporary. Contemporary worship is built around the praise-and-worship model, borrowed from the charismatic tradition of the twentieth century. If your church scored high on the green scale, you probably have a more experiential orientation in your worship structure, in that congregational singing is planned around a song list, which is ordered by mood or emotional flow rather than the event orientation of a traditional church. The songs may generally start with expressive praise, and then progress to intimate worship (hence, the term "praise-and-worship"). The atmosphere and attire tend to be informal, with a great degree of spontaneity in the planning.

What the green scale does not indicate, however, is **how** contemporary your church is. What is "contemporary" is always temporary, and it changes, by definition of the word itself. So, what is "contemporary" today? Many churches today view themselves as "contemporary," but really are singing keyboard-driven choruses from the 1980s, with lyrical melodies and rhyming lyrics. If so, they are really "classic" contemporary churches, taking a mostly Baby Boomer approach to the assembly. (*See* Chapter 5 for more description of Boomer worship).

The new generation of "contemporary" requires a new approach to stay current. So, we might need to invent a new term: "Postcontemporary." Postcontemporary churches are more trendy, less presentation-oriented, and more technology-driven. Postcontemporary worship style goes way beyond the hymns-versus-chorus debate. The songs themselves break the "rules" of what are now traditional choruses, and form a new subspecies of choruses: simple, grinding songs with an edge, which are guitar-driven, repetitive and somewhat unpolished and asymmetrical. Postcontemporary worship is eclectic, and (ironically) finds new ideas in historical multisensory worship, in certain ancient Celtic ideas, and in eastern religions. In radically postcontemporary worship, you might see icons, smell incense, and experience free chant or other pseudoancient borrowings. The style must appear to be authentic, uncontrived, and relational. What is the best label for this new style? Many churches call this Post-Modern Worship, or GenX Worship.

Red: Thematic

Churches that score high in the red factor are structured thematically in their worship. Thematic worship is more instructional in intent, with a stronger educational orientation than of those of experience or event. Many "seeker services" are thematic, with the music, drama, and spoken transitions all geared around a central message. If you scored in the moderate or high range on the red scale, the sermon topic is probably the focus of your worship activities. In their purest form, thematic assemblies can be seen more as creative educational presentations, or as performance, than as corporate worship. Thematic worship can be found in traditional or contemporary settings. It requires much more careful planning and repertoire than do the other two primary styles of worship.

Blue/Green: Blended Traditional

Blue/green blended worship can be described as a traditional form (with what we called event orientation above), with choruses blended in with the hymns and gospel songs. Some of the churches may even use choruses almost exclusively, but the structure is more traditional. In other words, the left column of the bulletin is still very similar week to week, because the structure is built around the events of the worship order, but the "flavor" of the music is more contemporary than in true "blue" worship.

Green/Blue: Blended Contemporary

Green/blue blended worship uses the praise and worship format, but blends hymns into the mix of songs used. The atmosphere can be formal or informal, the instrumentation may vary greatly, but green / blue worship is structured around *mood* rather than *rite*. Thus, adherence to an "order of worship" is flexible, but the overall "flavor" of the music is blended with classic hymns.

WHITE: PURPOSEFUL

If your church scored moderate to high on all three charts, you are experiencing what may be called "purposeful" worship, which is three-dimensional blended worship. "Purposeful" worship is studied and balanced between contemporary, traditional, and thematic. Churches that worship purposefully constantly study biblical, liturgical, theological, and practical aspects of worship, rather than just doing what seems to "work" (or what seemed to work several years ago). Such churches also are balanced in that they freely borrow from all three of the major worship traditions. Purposeful worship is creative, renewed, free, flowing, participative, innovative, and communal. Purposeful churches are constantly reevaluating and renewing their worship practice, and they change as they explore worship together. All effective churches, regardless of their historical tradition, should seek to be more purposeful in their worship. What do purposeful churches need to be careful to avoid? Be careful that your innovations do not decay into "same-old" habits. Every church has traditions, even if your tradition is to be different every week! Watch out for spiritual pride, and that your choice of "all" traditions doesn't degenerate into a choice of "no" traditions (which is described below).

GRAY: "RUT-UAL"

It is possible that if you scored in this category, your worship tradition simply does not fit any of the typical molds of Restoration churches. Perhaps your worship is high church, or noninstrumental, or highly unusual on purpose. But generally, if you scored low on all three categories, your church is experiencing "rutual" worship, which is not dynamic; it is the opposite of purposeful worship. With thoughtless repetition, it maintains the status quo. There is no new learning and there is no yearning after a vibrant relationship with the Lord. This rigid worship fixation is the same as last year, and ten years ago; in fact, the only thing that changes in the worship from week to week is the number in the songbook (in traditional churches) or the titles of the song sets (in contemporary churches). Thoughtless rituals need reconsideration. Traditions, whether new or old, should be studied and purposeful, not perpetuated without thought and evaluation of their effectiveness in worshiping God. This "gray" worship is the inexorable result of pragmatism, when it ceases to "work" anymore.

What color is your assembly? Is it the color you would choose?

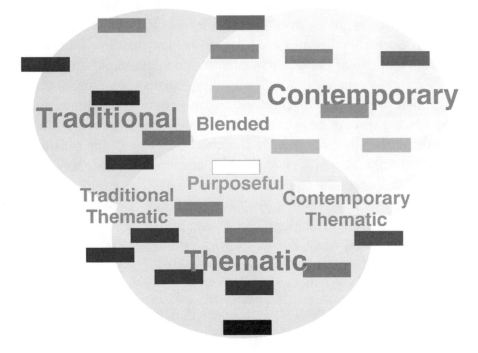

Step Four: What Is Our Focus? Weighing the Activities of Our Worship

When the church assembled in the New Testament, what did they do? We might identify seven different "givens" of New Testament worship.[1] They are:

Singing *(Eph. 5:19; Col. 3:16)*

Giving/Fellowship *(Acts 2:42; 1 Cor. 16:1,2; 2 Cor. 9:1,7)*

Lord's Table *(Acts 20:7; 1 Cor. 11:28,29)*

Lesson/Proclamation *(2 Tim. 4:1–5; 1 Cor. 14:3–5)*

Scripture Reading *(1 Tim. 4:3; Neh. 8,9)*

Prayer *(Acts 1:14; 2:42; 6:4,6; 10:9; 13:2,3)*

Evangelism *(1 Cor. 14:24,25)*

Now we get to a more narrative description of the emotional focus of your church assembly. Different congregations might make one of the elements more of an emotional focus than others in their assemblies. Note this: the seven worship styles identified here are not categorized by how much *time* they spend in a given activity, but rather how much that activity seems to receive *emotional focus.* For example, in a revival service 30 minutes might be given to a message and only 15 minutes to the invitation, but emotionally the entire service has been building toward that invitation, and no one doubts that it was the focus of the gathering.

So, which part of the assembly does your church seem to emphasize the most? Again, there is not necessarily a right or wrong answer, but it is good to know our set of values before we go advocating some new approach to renew our worship.

Some churches are **evangelistic**. Evangelistic churches emphasize evangelism and baptism, and they build their service toward the invitation. The service may be traditional or contemporary, and the response may be high pressure or low key, with walking the aisle or raising a hand quietly or filling out a card, but when the planning is done, it is with an evangelistic response in mind. Most likely, the Lord's Supper will be located before the message, so that the service can culminate in baptisms rather than an activity for Christians only. Note this: churches may or may not *say* that their services are built around the invitation; we are seeking the perceived practical emotional focus here.

Up until the 1960s and 1970s, almost every church of Christ, Christian church, Baptist, or other evangelical church structured their assembly evangelistically. Churches might sing six stanzas of "Just As I Am" as long as people were still responding while they sang. In between each verse the preacher would admonish the folk or tell a touching story to encourage another soul to respond by coming forward while the congregation sang. Not many churches are like that anymore.

There is a new model that is still evangelism-based, however. It is often called the Willow Creek model of seeker services, or seeker events. Ironically, at Willow Creek Community Church, they don't even use an "invitation." They don't want to try to get an emotional decision from people, so they calmly explain the gospel and invite people to "hang around" after the service is over to talk. Even though the approach is low key, the service is definitely geared toward that moment at the end of the service when seekers would come up to ask questions, and perhaps decide for Christ.

Other churches emphasize **singing** as the emotional focus of what they do. Some structure their singing around a song book, but most are of the newer "praise and worship" tradition. Increasingly, evangelical churches are buying into the model of believers (and seekers) together expressing themselves in praise and worship. Mostly such churches use contemporary choruses, with emotions ebbing and flowing as the congregation is led by a "worship leader" who guides them through "worship sets" of songs. Publishing houses such as Maranatha!, Integrity, and Vineyard are supplying this new, expressive, emotional, nonrational approach to the assembly.

Not many churches place their primary emotional emphasis on **Scripture reading**. However, those which come from the Reformation tradition have historically taken a rationalistic approach to their faith, and emphasize expository, rational explanation and application of the Word of God as the center of their assemblies.

Very few churches likewise place their primary emphasis on community **prayer**. Yet, Jesus said that the temple was intended to be called a house of prayer (Matt. 21:13; Isa. 56:7), and there are churches today who call themselves houses of prayer. But most church assemblies are not geared around prayer as the emotional center of why they gather on Sunday morning. In fact, in most churches' midweek prayer meetings have been replaced with midweek Bible studies, and those have in recent days been in turn replaced with midweek celebration services. There is a serious trend away from public prayer in many evangelical churches.

Many churches place primary emphasis on **preaching**. In many Christian church assemblies, perhaps twelve minutes are given to congregational singing, and a total of another 12 to 20 minutes to all of the other activities (prayer, Lord's Supper, offering, special music, drama, even announcements), but 30 or more minutes of time is needed for the message. The title of preference for many ministers is "preacher," implying that preaching is the most important thing he does. In fact, many evangelical churches call their assembly a "preaching service," a concept taken from the Roman Catholic *Prone*, a service which featured preaching but no Eucharist.

Some churches place emotional emphasis on **fellowship**. Most of these churches might be considered "body life" or "testimony" or "ministry" oriented. There is much emphasis on benevolence and meeting needs. They often sit in a circle to represent their unity and share with each other. Many fellowship-oriented churches are built around small groups, and their assemblies reinforce the relationships of those groups. Some churches have an altar call that emphasizes "ministry" (laying on of hands, prayer, counseling rooms, etc.) while the rest of the congregation prays for them and sings. All of these options emphasize that the central purpose of the church is not listening but participating.

There are a few churches that emphasize the **Lord's Supper**. Traditionally, Restoration Movement churches have used a rhetoric that indicates the Table is the center of their assembly (citing Acts 20:7 and other texts), but in practice, little attention, creativity, time, or emotional energy is spent on their gathering around the Table. Some liturgical churches, such as Orthodox and Roman Catholics, definitely have the Eucharist as the climax of their assemblies.

Later in this book, we will explore these seven elements of the worship assembly again. When we do, we will be seeking ways to

improve each of the areas. For now, though, we are merely identi-
fying how your church approaches each element in its practice.

Assessing These Elements

Which of the seven elements of public worship does your
church seem to emphasize the most? Rank each of the seven, based
on emotional focus (remember, this is not amount of time, but
what most of your people would consider the emotional focus of
your assembly).

Figure 2.6 Ranking the Seven Aspects of the Assembly

Activity	Rank of Emotional Focus (1-7):
Singing	____
Giving / Fellowship	____
Lord's Table	____
Lesson / Proclamation	____
Scripture Reading	____
Prayer	____
Evangelism	____

Step Five: Our Seeker Sensitivity Quotient: Measuring Our Outreach in Worship

You have, by this point, gone through four assessments of
your church. You have done a time breakdown, looked at your
demographic makeup, identified your church's "color" of worship
style, and determined the focus of its assembly. Now we turn to
your church's "seeker sensitivity quotient."

Most evangelical churches recognize the importance of the
Great Commission (Matt. 28:18-20) in their life and mission. So, to
what degree is the assembly at your church accomplishing the
Great Commission? Is it geared for the seeker, who may not know

the routines and practices of the church, or does it make a seeker feel like an outsider? Chapter 3 will deal with this issue from the philosophical perspective. First, we want to describe what *is*, then later help you decide what *should* be.

UNDERSTANDING TERMINOLOGY

An **unchurched person** is someone who has not been exposed to the "church" subculture. The person may be a believer who was won to Christ through an individual or in a small group. More often the person is not yet a believer, and may or may not be a *seeker*.

A **seeker** is a person who is spiritually interested or is searching. The person may or may not be "churched," and may or may not be a convert, but the seeker is searching for spiritual truth.

A **churched person**, then, is someone who is familiar with the ways and means of the culture of the organization we often call "church." The person may or may not be a believer, but the churched blend in with the members.

A **seeker event** or **seeker service** is the modern-day reinvention of an evangelistic revival service. In its purest form, it is an assembly specifically designed to present the gospel to the seeker. "Seeker-sensitive worship" is a service designed not to offend the unchurched.

Figure 2.7 Seeker Sensitivity Self-Assessment

Here is a series of statements. For each, answer on a scale of 1-5, according to this scale: 1 = disagree strongly, 2 = disagree slightly, 3 = neither agree nor disagree, 4 = agree slightly, 5 = agree strongly. Add up your scores and find your seeker sensitivity quotient.

1. Everything we do in the assembly is geared for the unchurched.   1 2 3 4 5
2. Our guests find the best parking spaces.   1 2 3 4 5
3. We provide helpful printed material for the first-timer.   1 2 3 4 5
4. Directions to classrooms and restrooms are clearly marked.   1 2 3 4 5
5. Our nursery is always ready for more.   1 2 3 4 5
   (Adequate beds, toys, workers, systematic record for allergies and other special needs, organized method of protecting and giving attention to each child in our care.)
6. We leave prime seats available for the latecomer.   1 2 3 4 5
7. We do not have any religious symbolism in our worship center,   1 2 3 4 5
   as it might be confusing or meaningless to an unchurched person.
8. People come dressed casually. Someone who owns only jeans and   1 2 3 4 5
   T-shirts would not feel out of place.

9. There is an overriding sense of tolerance and welcome for people 1 2 3 4 5
of any lifestyle.

10. We avoid all "insider" terminology and humor. 1 2 3 4 5

11. Announcements are aimed at newcomers, rather than members. 1 2 3 4 5

12. We use high-resolution graphics and design in our printed materials. 1 2 3 4 5

13. We spend very little time in our gatherings doing things 1 2 3 4 5
uncomfortable to the unchurched visitor
(prayer, singing unfamiliar songs, communion, offering, etc.).

14. We spend very little time in emotionally "down" tempo. 1 2 3 4 5

15. Our music is of excellent quality, and it does not sound like it 1 2 3 4 5
belongs to an earlier era.

16. Our means of inviting a seeker to the gospel is clear and authentic. 1 2 3 4 5

17. We address the seeker directly rather than making a visitor feel 1 2 3 4 5
like he or she is just "listening in."

18. We give clear instructions for newcomers, such as in singing 1 2 3 4 5
(What's a hymnal?), Bible reading *(What page is that?)*, communion *(How and why are they doing this? Am I invited?)*, and giving *(Are these dues, or some sort of admission charge? Am I expected to give?)*.

19. We regularly survey our first-time guests. 1 2 3 4 5

20. We modify what we do based on their impressions. 1 2 3 4 5

21. We follow up on everyone who wishes it. 1 2 3 4 5

22. Our members feel that they can invite unchurched people 1 2 3 4 5
to the assembly.

23. Most newcomers have been brought by members. 1 2 3 4 5

24. The overall mood of the service is positive and upbeat. 1 2 3 4 5

Total seeker-sensitivity score *(add values for statements 1–24):* _____

KEY:

Raw score	Avg./question	Assessment
24-40	1.0-1.6	Our church has made a clear choice not to use Sunday morning for outreach.
41-71	1.7-2.9	Perhaps we occasionally aim for seeker sensitivity, but mostly we do not.
72-95	3.0-3.9	We have made some choices to include seekers, but have not made consistent choices about outreach.
96-109	4.0-4.5	We are above average in our quest to evangelize during the assembly.
110-120	4.6-5.0	We are highly committed to evangelism, and have taken clear steps to carry it out in our weekend assemblies.

Where do you lie on this spectrum? Make a mark on this line, based on the raw score from above. Does it seem accurate?

Believers-oriented		-O-		Seekers-oriented
24	48	72	96	120

Fiɲal Step:
Svmmary aɲd Application

Now that we have done five exercises assessing the worship at your church, let's summarize and draw some conclusions. Remember (this is important), to a degree, there is no "wrong" answer; these tools are merely to help you identify your values. This is merely a measurement of where your church currently stands, not of where you want it to be.

Step One: Our Time Budget
What are your apparent values as a church, based on how you actually spend your time?
Do you agree with these values?
Are your observations consistent with what you want?

Step Two: Our Demographic Chart
What kind of people does your church reach, based on who is actually there?
Are these the people you feel called to reach?
Are your findings consistent with what you want?

Step Three: Our Worship Color
What are your worship values, according to the worship "color" exercise?
Would everyone at your church agree with these values?
Are your findings consistent with what you want?

Step Four: Our Activity Focus
Which element(s) of the assembly does your church tend to emphasize the most?

Which element do you think they neglect the most?

Are your findings consistent with what you want?

Step Five: Our Outreach Quotient

On the spectrum of believers-oriented to seekers-oriented, where does your assembly fall?

Is this finding accurate?

Are your findings consistent with what you want?

Summary Narrative

Now, do a narrative. Describe in a paragraph what you see to be the greatest strength and greatest need in your assembly.

Now that you, and perhaps a group of others, have scrutinized your assemblies, you get to the most important part of the assessment process: application. Discuss your various findings and conclusions as a group. Don't allow the discussion to become an argument; keep it on the level of an objective assessment.

The next step is to pray together (Seriously! For an hour or more!). Seek the Lord for guidance and unity regarding your values and your actions. Where do you sense the Lord calling you to go from here? If there is disagreement at this stage, simply pass over that matter and move on to the next.

Finally, it is time to take action on the areas of consensus that arise from these discussions. Choose two or three things in which you have strong agreement, and create a plan for how to carry out the changes.

A word of warning: *Don't try to change too much, and don't run ahead of the congregation. Also, be sure to read the rest of this book before you make any changes you will regret!*

PART TWO

Discovering Where We Want to Be

CHAPTER THREE
TARGETING OUR WORSHIP

WHERE IS THE TARGET, AND HOW CAN WE HIT IT?

So far, our work has been to identify the pattern and values that already exist in your church's worship. Now we turn to what you would like the worship to become in the future. For this exercise, we will be making some hard choices. So let's set the background first.

HAS WORSHIP BEGUN YET?

One apocryphal Sunday morning I was standing at the back door greeting people as they entered. Someone else was leading the early part of the service, and I was feeling no rush. A man ran breathlessly in with his wife, two minutes late for the start of the morning assembly. As the young man shook my hand he whispered, "Has worship begun yet?"

"Oh yes," I said, "From the foundations of the world, the heavens have been declaring the glory of God. The sky has proclaimed the work of His hands. That's found in Psalm 19, you know."

I could see that he was not looking for that as an answer. So I continued, "Oh, you mean, 'Have *people* begun to worship yet?' Yes, everyone worships. The only question for us is whether that worship is acceptable to God or not. We all worship—we all hold something up as of highest value to us. To some it's a false god of money, people, fame, power, or pleasure. For others it is the one true God, but they harbor selfishness or bitterness in their hearts, so their worship of the one true God is still unacceptable. But ultimately, yes, everyone worships."

He was a little embarrassed and somewhat unamused, and showed some signs of being a little miffed. But he was also a little more enlightened, I reasoned to myself.

"Right," he said, "but that's not what I meant. I meant, 'Has church started yet?'"

"Oh, that's different," I said. "The church has been around for about 2000 years now, with Jesus Christ as the Chief Cornerstone. It is built on the foundation of the apostles and prophets, and the gates of hell cannot prevail against it. Jesus Himself said so, you know."

"I mean," he hissed, "has our church worship service begun yet?"

"Well, hopefully, since 1995 we have been successfully offering to God our sacrifices and service in an acceptable way. You know, Hebrews 13:15-16 says that we are to continually offer to God a sacrifice of praise, the fruit of lips that confess His name. And do not forget to do good and share with others, for with such sacrifices God is pleased. So confessing His name, doing good, and sharing with others are our services of worship."

At this point, I discerned in my spirit that this man was not interested in learning more about worship from me. His wife at that point had looked through the doors and said, "You know, I don't think worship has begun yet."

She may have been right. So, let me ask you: Has worship begun yet? For you? And how do you know when it starts? Why do we gather here on the first day of the week? How do we know when we are pleasing God with what we do on Sunday mornings at church? These are the questions we will address in this chapter and the next.

Worship as a Target

Some have said people are changed when God "shows up." He "showed up" in 2 Chronicles 5, when Solomon dedicated the temple. The temple was filled with smoke from the glory of His presence. He "showed up" in Acts 2, on the Day of Pentecost, when what seemed to be tongues of fire separated and rested on the believers. But, how do we know when God "shows up" today? Can His presence be measured or seen? Can we plan for it? Is it subjective and individual, or is there an objective and corporate manifestation? If true worship is our target, what is the center of the target? How can we know we hit a bull's-eye?

Finding the Bull's-Eye

Let's pursue this analogy of a target. A bull's-eye occurs when true worship takes place. Many worship leaders think, "if only we would change the order of the service," or, "if we just had more contemporary music," or, "we could add drama or more banners or more creativity, and that will make worship happen." But it won't. Changing the trappings can make the environment more conducive for worship, to be sure. But don't start there. Worship happens in the heart, not in the program. In truth, the heart of the worshiper is the target, and only God knows when a bull's-eye is scored.

A leader can't make worship happen any more than a farmer can make a horse drink. You know the old saying, "You can lead a horse to water, but you can't make him drink"? So it is with worship. You can create the right setting, say all the right words, and do all the right actions to lead someone in worship, but if the heart isn't worshiping, worship hasn't happened. On the other hand, a really "bad" worship service can score a bull's-eye if your heart is right with God.

You can worship while riding a subway, while playing golf, or while going through great personal distress. So you can worship at church, even at *your* church, this Sunday morning. Understand this deep down before we go any further, because the rest of this book deals with those outward trappings, and it would be easy to get out of balance.

Well, as the amendment to the saying goes, you may not be able to make a horse drink water, but you can salt his oats. When he gets thirsty enough, he will choose to drink. In the same way, words and actions can help influence a heart to worship. The job of worship leading is simply to get the obstructions out of the way, and thus to make the act of public prayer a heartfelt choice.

From another viewpoint, we can start with the heart and define our target from the inside out. If my heart is right with God, it will cause me to do what will glorify the One my heart yields its allegiance to, including public worship. A right heart causes me to have right words and actions, and having right words and actions helps me to have a right heart. It is a sacred cause and effect which a wise leader will understand before leading others in worship.

Worship renewal is as difficult to define as a warm heart. The Father is seeking worshipers who will worship in spirit and in truth, and He alone knows when He has found one. The heart of the worshiper is the target, the Spirit is the renewal agent, and the assembly should be a reflection of the life that wells up from inside.

THE SEARCH FOR "REAL" WORSHIP

How can a church know when it has achieved its goal of "real" worship when there are so many choices and models available? Could we mistakenly think we are in the center of what God intends for our assemblies when in reality we have missed the mark? In the previous chapter, I stressed that there is no "right" pattern for worship and that different approaches or emphases are not necessarily better. Perhaps more accurately, I believe that all of the approaches in the last chapter hit the target. But in this section I want to probe for the center. Is it possible to hit the target, yet not score a bull's-eye? If so, what might a "near miss" look like?

THE GOD OF THE BURNING BUSH

On the far side of the desert, at Horeb, the mountain of God,

. . . the angel of the LORD appeared to [Moses] in flames of fire from within a bush. Moses saw that though the bush was on fire it did not burn up. So Moses thought, "I will go over and see this strange sight—why the bush does not burn up."

When the LORD saw that he had gone over to look, God called to him from within the bush, "Moses, Moses!"

And Moses said, "Here I am."

"Do not come any closer," God said. "Take off your sandals, for the place where you are standing is holy ground." Then he said, "I am the God of your father, the God of Abraham, the God of Isaac and the God of Jacob." At this, Moses hid his face, because he was afraid to look at God.

The LORD said, "I have indeed seen the misery of my people in Egypt. I have heard them crying out because of their slave drivers, and I am concerned about their suffering. So I have come down to rescue them. . . . So now, go. I am sending you to Pharaoh to bring my people the Israelites out of Egypt" (Exod. 3:1-10).

When the Lord revealed Himself to Moses, He used a burning bush. The bush brought interest and then fear in Moses, as the Lord identified Himself, then issued a call He wanted Moses to fulfill.

What if the Lord used the bush today?

WORSHIP IS MORE THAN EMOTION

Some worship leaders emphasize the *emotion* of worship. If you dance and laugh and cry and raise your hands and fall to the ground, is that true worship? Is worship leading a process of leading people through the right moods in a convincing way?

On a practical level, certain emotions can become associated with the presence of God. The center of the target is then to experience "the Presence." Real worship does engage the emotions and does involve the Lord's presence, but emotions must never be the central goal. Emotions can be engaged at a secular concert or a movie. To equate worship with a certain spiritual mood is to accept a near-miss substitute instead of the real thing.

Jesus said that worship needs to be both in spirit and in truth (John 4:24). As worship leaders, we miss the mark if we aim for the emotions of worship but neglect the truth of worship in the process.

Tommy Tenney suggests[1] that if God spoke in a burning bush today, some churches might be guilty of gathering week by week to dance around the bush. They come to experience the Great Miraculous Burning, and perhaps some even bring matches to ensure that the bush will burn on command. They are too busy celebrating to hear the voice of God call out, "Do not come any closer. Take off your sandals, for the place where you are standing is holy ground."

Remember, Jesus "shows up" whenever His people are gathered in His name. He promises that He is here, whether we "feel" Him or not. Sometimes the emotions are there, and sometimes they are not. Wise worship leaders are not seduced by the siren's call to reproduce last Sunday's emotional moment, or the mood set at the last conference they attended. Wise worship leaders remember what the center of the target is.

You may find success by leading people through certain emotions of worship; people may flock to the assemblies to experience the touch of God. But emotional manipulation misses the center of the target of true worship.

WORSHIP IS MORE THAN EVANGELISM

Still other churches conclude that the center of the assembly is *evangelism*, and that converts are the real agenda for Sunday morning. Many build their worship theology around John 12:32, where Jesus said, "And I, if I be lifted up from the earth, will draw all men unto me" (KJV). Of course, Jesus was talking about being crucified, not being worshiped, yet that is overlooked in many songs and in the worship evangelism philosophy of many worship leaders.

To use the burning bush analogy again, these churches might be concerned that flames could intimidate or frighten a newcomer. So they douse the bush with water, or perhaps cover the light, or maybe issue free sunglasses to visitors. They talk about the bush, and let the uninitiated know that there is a bush, and that someday they might wish to see the flame. But remember this: Moses was a newcomer to burning bushes, too. God rudely initiated contact with him, and he discovered that the call of God is never palatable or easy.

Many churches use the traditional evangelical model, with the Baptismal Service as the intended climax of the assembly. Other churches follow the new Seeker Event model, with a low-key, felt-needs, topical message. Those who receive Jesus (the word "repent" is seldom used) do not have to go public with their decision. But the goal of both approaches is fulfilling the Great Commission in the assembly. Some of these churches grow, and lives are being changed. Certainly, they are glorifying God by their evangelism. But are they worshiping? Or is an evangelistic service another substitute for worship?

People's needs may be met in a seeker event. But what about *God's* needs? We want to be seeker-sensitive in our assemblies. Whatever happened to *God*-sensitive worship? We poll our unchurched neighbors for worship ideas; how about sending one of our polls to the Lord Almighty to ask Him what He is looking for in worship? Know this for certain: The Father is seeking true worshipers (John 4:23). Seeker events may be evangelistic crusades, harvest meetings, Sunday morning revivals, or presentations of the gospel, but might not be true worship.

Here is a challenge for seeker-oriented churches: do not issue promises to people that can't be kept. If I provide spiritual and practical principles to help someone deal with stress, for example, I may have allowed them to go to hell more comfortably! If they apply certain scriptural principles, but miss the first point—regeneration through the Holy Spirit—they might not have the power or ability to apply the rest of the points. Let us never counterfeit true Christianity by teaching people Christian character or Christian principles without first giving them Christ!

If you are leading an evangelism-based service, or a self-improvement-based assembly, you could be teaching scriptural principles, your church may be growing, you might truly help people, and crowds are flocking to it. Something is happening at your church, but it might not be worship.

Worship Is More Than Education

Still other churches think that the assembly is where folks come to learn something new about the Lord. The sermon becomes the center of the gathering; a one-way proclamation of truth provides the theme of the singing, the prayers, the drama, and all of the spoken transitions.

I describe this thematic approach to the assembly as *creative education*. Whether aimed at the seeker or at the maturing believer, the focus of the gathering is the topic of the day. Planning teams are given the basic theme weeks or months in advance, then set out creatively to prepare people to hear the proclamation and take home the challenge of the lesson for the day.

Creative education churches in effect erect a monument to the Burning Bush. In their edifice they sing and study and talk about The Bush That Once Was. After the meeting, as they leave they comment, "Lovely bush this morning, Preacher. Inspiring description of the flame." He humbly replies, "Thank you." And so, rather than revealing the Glory, the bush becomes a topic of polite discussion. The Presence of God does not fit our polite guidelines. The burning bush was for a purpose, and on seeing it we fall, afraid to look, shaken and changed, until He lifts us up and sends us out.

If your church assembly centers on thematic, education-driven worship style, it may be growing, people's lives may be changed, and there may be a wonderful sense of expectancy each Lord's Day. The mood among the people may be positive, the program may be excellent and creative, and people may come away every week with a new lesson to apply to their lives to the glory of God. Thus their lives become acceptable and fragrant offerings of worship to the Lord. But the question here is, has the assembly itself hit a bull's-eye of worship? Or is it another near-miss? Learning new information is not the center of worship. It may be excellent creative education, but it can also be a counterfeit for real worship.

Worship Is More Than Entertainment

Still other churches get the rockin' band and current technology and light shows and dramatic sketches, and present a polished and professional package from beginning to end. Or, in a different style, they hire professional musicians for their choir and have an organist/choirmaster and use high quality musicians in string quartets and other cultured musical expressions. Such an *entertainment orientation* can cause a church to grow and people to be psyched for the assembly, and it may even glorify God. But did worship really happen?

Do you know how to improve your singing? Don Hustad describes how to guarantee great sound in your song service. He says you must get a great sound system, have a great-sounding contemporary band, and then put four singers up front as a worship team, each with microphone in hand. Rehearse the music so it is excellent. That is guaranteed to improve the sound of your song service. The *congregation* may not be singing—but it will sound good anyway! Or, in a different style, choir and orchestra could create a great musical sound. In either style, the congregation is actually optional in this package, because the sound happens whether they participate or not.

Worship must include congregational involvement, or it is a near-miss. To be sure, worship leaders must be sensitive to those who cannot participate for one reason or another. But the norm, and a worthy goal, is still congregational involvement. If worship is our target, participation is the goal.

Many of us get worship and entertainment confused. Both may make use of quality music, which is focused on God. Both can employ creative use of the arts. But hear this: Worship is more akin to work than it is to entertainment. (That's why they call it a worship *service!*) Our spiritual service of worship is to present our bodies to Him. Hebrews 13:15 says, "Through Jesus, therefore, let us continually offer to God *a sacrifice of praise*—the fruit of lips that confess his name." Worship is a sacrifice. Remember what David said? "I will not offer to the Lord what costs me nothing." Worship is work, and worship is costly. Entertaining programs may edify, and easy worship may draw, but if it involves no sacrifice, it is not worship. When Moses heard the voice of God, he ceased being intrigued and hid his face, afraid to look at the One who was speaking. True worship takes discipline, consecration, and prayer. And prayer is not easy.

If you have been leading in any of these "near-miss" assemblies, your church may have all the trappings of success. People may be moved emotionally, folks may be creatively educated, souls may be won evangelistically, crowds may be entertained, and your church may be growing. But are they worshiping? Or is emotion, education, evangelism, or entertainment serving as a near-miss substitute for worship? You may not be hitting the center of the target of worship. It's not that worship is not happening at all, but you could have missed the center of the target, and taken a counterfeit instead of the real thing.

Worship Celebrates Christ!

The Lord is still the Great I AM of the burning bush. But in these last days, God has not revealed Himself through a burning bush; He has revealed Himself to us through His Son, Jesus Christ (Heb. 1:1,2).

Perhaps by now I have offended everyone, one at a time. I have said everything that I think worship is *not*. So what is the real thing? What is *real* worship? If all those approaches to worship have not hit a bull's-eye, what *does*? Robert Webber suggests it this way: *true worship celebrates Christ*. We do more than study truth or feel emotions; we celebrate the Lord Jesus Christ Himself. The center of our target has to do with the birth, life, death, burial, resurrection, ascension, reign, and return of Jesus. Through drama, storytelling, pageantry, symbolism, music, Scripture reading, meditation, testimonies, giving, sharing, and prayer, everything in worship somehow is centered in Christ, who is our life. By this we express God's worth by celebrating the work of God's Son. If we miss Christ in the midst of our assembly, we have missed worship. If somehow in the course of Sunday morning it does not become very clear whom we are celebrating, we have not really worshiped.

Christianity is not a philosophy that we have accepted; it is a person. We come, not just to encourage other humans, but to point one another to the Son of God. Our salvation was bought, not by a well-meaning but misdirected rabbi of centuries ago, but by the One who gave Himself as atoning sacrifice for our sins. Our life is hidden in Christ, not in a doctrinal hope. Faith is not positive or possibility thinking; it is rooted in Christ Jesus, and if it is not, it is not biblical faith. And so we celebrate, not a religion, and not a concept; we celebrate the life, death, and resurrection of the Lord Jesus Christ. That is worship, it is the gospel, and it is the center of the target: Christ Jesus; anything else is something less.

WHAT DOES CELEBRATION LOOK LIKE?

So, how do we *celebrate* Jesus? Does that mean that we have a party? Does it mean a solemn assembly? Does it mean a series of readings? Perhaps it would help to think about other celebrations in our lives: graduations, anniversaries, birthdays, championships, or holidays. Our celebrations take on different moods and forms for different occasions.

At our house, when we celebrate a child's birthday, there are certain rituals that we look forward to every year. Even if they are repetitive traditions, most do not lose their meaning with the repetition. You probably have your own rituals. On those special days, you look backward, you celebrate the moment, and perhaps you look ahead. But mostly, you consecrate the day for the person who is the object of your celebration.

Is that celebration full of tradition? Certainly it is. Is it full of joviality and loud music? It is not, for the most part. It is celebration because it is set apart (sanctified) in our hearts to honor one person. And through decorations, pageantry, storytelling, gifts, a meal, and the presence of special loved ones, the day is a favorite.

The only way to ruin a birthday is to forget the guest of honor, or to celebrate with no forethought and only a sense of obligation.

And so I say it again: let's celebrate Christ Jesus!

It's All about Jesus!

I make such a big deal about the matter of finding the center of the target (the worshiper's heart) and hitting a bull's-eye (celebrating Jesus) because it is so easy to forget. The Lord is our song, Christ Jesus is our refuge, God is our salvation, and in the Lord Jesus Christ is our forgiveness. I guess I feel a need to clarify because otherwise you might come to the wrong conclusion. It's all supposed to be about Jesus, but if you sing the most popular songs today, you might get the wrong idea. Let me explain myself.

Do you get the feeling that we enjoy singing about our feelings about God more than we actually identify Him? That we sing more about mercy and less about Jesus who is the source of mercy?

A student looked through a collection compiled by a major publisher of the most popular choruses used in churches today.[2] In the collection, the word "mercy" appears 16 times, while "Jesus" appears only 14 times. Our gospel is all about Jesus, but perhaps some people are thinking that the center of the gospel is all about *mercy*, rather than about *Him*!

Compare that to the New Testament epistles. The review of an exhaustive concordance reveals that the word "Jesus" appears 341 times, but "mercy" only 38 times.[3] Perhaps we should learn from the balance that the Holy Spirit gave us in the Bible, and remember that the One who bought our salvation is more worthy of our attention than the mercy itself.

What I have come to call "creeping liberalism" is a problem in churches today. Many are not overt liberals who question the validity of the Scriptures. But sometimes we simply leave out the controversial in an attempt to be seeker sensitive. We have purposed not to be offensive, lest we turn people away before we've had a chance to preach the Good News to them. But the gospel is the Good News of Jesus Christ, not the Good News of Mercy.

Week after week goes by, and slowly it dawns on us that we have not preached or sung about the blood of Christ, about the cross, or about repentance for months—not because we don't believe in them anymore, but because they never seem to be appropriate. If we never get around to the hard truths—the glorious truths—of the gospel, have we given the full truth? Jesus' one-word sermon was "Repent!" What is ours?

Worship renewal is taking place in our country—praise the Lord! But it seems our worship renewal has more to do with musical style and emotional expression than it does truth. The current trend in worship songs is intimate adoration of an often-unspecified deity. But in many "contemporary churches" we never get around to singing doctrine. Jesus told us that the Father was seeking those who would worship Him in spirit and in truth.

Most evangelical churches have tended to err on an overemphasis of the "truth" side, but have lacked spirit. We have become Christians "from the neck up" in many cases. That has needed correction! But I'm afraid that now the pendulum has already swung past center, and that many of our worship planners have led us to imbalance the other way.

Someone needs to call us back to Christ-centered truth. One of my favorite song lyrics of years past is "One Day." The music is dated by today's standards, but the words are a gold mine.[4] In its refrain, we express the fullness of The Christ Event:

> Living—He loved me,
> Dying—He saved me,
> Buried—He carried my sins far away;
> Rising—He justified freely, forever:
> One day He's coming—O glorious day!"[5]

Similarly, I applaud the newer version of The Christ Event in song as written more recently by Rick Founds in "Lord, I Lift Your Name on High," which traces Jesus' path from heaven, to earth, to the cross, then the grave, and ascension to the sky—the full gospel in a mere five lines.

These are the kinds of songs we need. We need writers to cre-

ate songs like these. We also need worship leaders to fill our congregational singing with songs like these.

It's all about Jesus, you know. It's about His life, His teachings,
His atoning sacrifice, His resurrection, His exalted position, and His
return. The greatest commandment is to love the Lord your God
with all of your heart, with all your soul, with all your mind, and
with all your strength. Church is not just a party over the death
of guilt; it is a celebration of the Lord Jesus Christ. O come, let us
adore *Him—Christ, the Lord!*

Pursuing the Presence

Many Christians define worship as entering the Presence of
God. It seems to be the assumption of the purpose of the assembly
itself. If so, pursuing the Presence is the most important thing we can
do when we gather. But *how* we sense the Presence is widely diverse.

The Experiential Presence

Some believers define the Presence **experientially**. They
might construct their worship around the pattern of entering His
gates with thanksgiving and His courts with praise, and move all
the way to entering into the Most Holy Place. There, they see the
smoke or sense some other manifestation of the physical presence
of the Lord. Their primary approach to worship is represented by
the Greek verb *proskuneo*, and they bow and adore.[7]

Have you ever experienced "The Presence"? If so, what was it
like? Did the person next to you also experience it? Did you wave
your arm as if moving smoke to help sense it? Did music help to
bring it in? Has "The Presence" ever come when you were by yourself, not expecting it?

There is only one clear (and another ancillary) description in
the New Testament of a manifestation of God's Spirit. On the Day
of Pentecost, the disciples were all together in one accord, having
prayed for ten days. They were waiting for "power."

I wonder what they expected to happen in that upper room? Whatever they expected, they saw nothing of any consequence until the Day of Pentecost had fully come. Then God came in His perfect, sovereign timing. There was no mistaking it, for there was a visible sign, and a miraculous language.

Do you think they were surprised by what happened when the Spirit suddenly came? The event was duplicated at the house of Cornelius. There, Peter was definitely taken by surprise that the Spirit should be poured out on Gentiles just as it had been on the Jewish disciples at Pentecost. God made Himself manifest by His sovereign will.

Whatever form it takes, the Presence is experiential for these believers. For some, the very goal of the assembly is to "enter His presence," or, rather, have The Presence manifest itself in the midst of the saints.

THE SACRAMENTAL PRESENCE

Other believers have a more objective definition of the presence. While they may agree with their experiential brothers about entering the Presence during Sunday assemblies, their concept of "the Presence" is **sacramental**. For some, the "real presence" of Christ is in the bread and wine, and the church is (literally) the Body of Christ. So, by attending the assembly, they come into "the Presence" by faith, with or without emotions or the physical senses substantiating what they know to be true.[8] Jesus promised that where two or three are gathered in His name, He is there. Jesus said the bread we break is His body, and the fruit of the vine is His blood. He is there!

Of course, there are certain dangers to this objective, sacramental approach to worship leading. Worship can become a thoughtless routine, objectively efficacious without personal faith on the part of the worshiper. The worship leader, too, can plan a service out of a book, read prayers someone else has written, and mean none of it.

The Continual Presence

Still others define the Presence more indirectly, as **lifestyle**. Jesus said that He would be with us always (Matt. 28:20), and we are to be filled continually with the Spirit (Eph. 5:18). We dwell in the Presence always, not in an experiential sense, and not in a sacramental sense, but in a real sense, nonetheless.

So maybe "entering the presence" is irrelevant. He is always here. The Holy Spirit was with us, but now He actually and literally indwells us (John 14:17). So to many saints, the whole terminology of "entering" is foreign. After all, we live and move and have our being in Him (Acts 17:28), God is everywhere, and we cannot (or should not, depending on your theology) leave His presence. So, we come to encourage one another, to sing to one another, to win the lost, and to give thanks and praise and worship, but not to "enter into" anything. This approach to worship is represented by the Greek verb *latreuo*; they serve and pray in the name of Jesus.

Can You Make "The Presence?"

Some people experience the manifest presence of God week by week, some don't. Two believers could be in the same meeting; one experiences a powerful sense of the Presence, another does not. But here is the good news: He is here, whether our personal experience tells us so or not. He promised, and He who promised is faithful. He is here. He is always here. He is in the fellowship, in the teaching, in the reading, in the bread, and in the fruit of the vine. He visits us when the music swirls and soars and the emotional setting is just right; and He is just as much present in a small group meeting, when two Christian friends pray together in a coffee shop, or in the silence of an underground house church in China.

Is the presence of God subjectively experienced, or is it objectively understood? It may not be an either/or matter. It can be both/and. He is objectively present, every day and in a special way in the assembly, and He may be subjectively felt as well. The Sovereign One can make Himself known at any time that He chooses.

Worship leaders are in danger when they try to "manufacture" the presence of God by drawing attention to it, by creating musical moments, or by seeking to make that "moment" happen week after week, as if our music or our praise will make God "come down." God is enthroned upon the praise of His people (Psalm 22:3), but it is flawed theology to think He must wait for our praises to reveal Him. Be careful not to craft the gift of God with human hands![9]

Whom Is Sunday Morning For?

One more topic as we refine the center of the target, and as we determine our values as a church: On whom is the focus of the worship?

This is a more difficult topic than it may seem at first. Worship and evangelism almost seem to be contradictory goals. How can I welcome unchurched guests at church, yet never water down the worship? Or, how can I experience the deep mysteries of Christ, yet not leave my unchurched friends out? I can become philosophically dysfunctional, stuck somewhere between wanting to serve people and still please God.

Which brings me to my question: Sunday morning is supposed to be for whom, anyway? Is it for God, for Christian people, or for the unchurched? Should we be looking up, looking out, or looking around during the service? Or can we do all three?

Unhappily, it seems that many churches have not thought much about this question, and so they have failed to succeed at any goal. They go through thoughtless rituals, their services have no appeal to modern culture, and their lackluster worship fails to attract the God of the universe. What is the answer? Whom is Sunday morning for?

Our Big Trilemma

The Church is facing a major trilemma today. Only slowly have I come to realize how big it is. This single issue may be behind most of the current debates about worship today. It is behind the debate over whether to limit a service to an hour and communion service to five minutes; behind the question of evening church services and the use of drama in the service; even behind the question of whether announcements and shaking hands belong in the morning worship assembly. This trilemma is also bigger than the controversial musical issues of the last two decades. It is bigger than the issue of dormant organs, replacing expensive sound systems, and remodeling sanctuaries; bigger than the issue of hymnals and projectors and blue jeans and drums; bigger than the issue of raising hands and clapping during singing.

The controversial trilemma is broader and more philosophical than any of these particulars. It is the question of *whom* the Sunday assembly is for. Whom do we meet for, primarily? Is it for man or for God? If it is for man, is it for believers or unbelievers, or both? If it is for God, how much do man's needs, wants, and desires come into play? In bigger words, is our worship to be theocentric (Christocentric) or anthropocentric?

ARE YOU THEOCENTRIC AND ANTHROPOCENTRIC?

What is meant by the terms "theocentric worship," and "anthropocentric worship"? It is not the *object* of worship, which is always Yahweh God in the name of the Lord Jesus Christ, through the empowerment of the Holy Spirit; rather, it is the *lens* through which that worship is filtered. Theocentric worship asks, "Does this please God?" Anthropocentric worship asks, "Is this meeting the needs of people?"[10]

Let me clarify that *quality* is not the issue here. A high degree of care and an emphasis on quality can drive any church. The issue is not the *quality*, but rather on whom the quality is *focused*. Do we do what we do because God deserves the very best (a theocentric focus), or because we want to meet people's needs (an anthropocentric focus)? Often it is impossible to sort through the mixed motives in our own hearts and discern the exact blend of why we choose to do something.

The people-centered approach is definitely the cutting edge of church growth ("We've got to stop answering questions that no one is asking!"). The God-centered approach is rooted more in the Christian heritage, and it seems to reflect integrity ("We will be true no matter what!"). Writers and spokesmen for both sides have provided passionate documentation to this challenge.

What makes the trilemma unresolvable in some ways is that it is impossible to be completely in one camp or another. Those who are so intent on pleasing God that they neglect people (a total theocentrist) will find that after a while no one comes to worship anymore, and God is not pleased with that. And those who ignore pleasing God (a total anthropocentrist) will wind up leaving the realm of worship altogether, for the flesh resists true worship. However, before we let our cultural conditioning or our emotions dictate our response, perhaps we should find out what Scripture has to say in this matter. When the first generation Christians met on the first day of the week, who was their assembly built around?

WHAT DOES THE BIBLE SAY?

What does the New Testament example provide for today's church? Were they primarily theocentric or anthropocentric? The answer may be a bit surprising. There is no record of actual church assemblies in the New Testament, but the passages that do refer to corporate gatherings are quite revealing.

My preconception was that studying Scripture would reveal clear theocentric worship in the New Testament assemblies. I assumed that a people-centered focus was a new development starting with evangelicals in America. However, there is good indication that worship in the New Testament was a mixture of both a people-centered and a God-centered orientation.

The first and clearest statement of early worship is Acts 2:42-47. It indicates a focus on **God** ("They devoted themselves to the apostles' teaching . . . to the breaking of bread and to prayer. . . . Praising God. . . ."), on **one another** (". . . and to the fellowship.

. . . All the believers were together and had everything in common. . . . Every day they continued to meet together in the temple courts. They broke bread in their homes and ate together . . ."), and also on **outsiders** (". . . they gave to anyone as he had need. . . . and enjoying the favor of all the people. And the Lord added to their number daily those who were being saved.")

In a rare account of the tenor of a public assembly, the apostle Paul instructs the Corinthian church in how to repair their meetings. Again, God and man are both represented in this passage, including having sensitivity for the unbelieving visitor. The emphasis here seems to come down strongest on the side of building up the church (1 Corinthians 14). Similarly, the two passages which may refer to congregational singing (Col. 3:16; Eph. 5:19) contain both God and people, as the churches are instructed to sing *to one another* (people) with psalms, hymns and spiritual songs, singing and making music in your hearts *to the Lord* (the focus being on the Lord). The Book of James gives indication also that visitors (perhaps unbelievers) are expected and should be treated correctly (Jas. 2:1-4). Certainly when the New Testament church gathered for worship, God was at the center of their thoughts; they met in His name and for the sake of worshiping Him. However, these references indicate that they also came together to honor Him by meeting the needs of one another and sharing the Good News with the "unchurched."

Perhaps this problem can best be resolved by observing the two most common words for worship in the New Testament: *proskuneo* and *latreuo.*

Proskuneo means "to kiss the hand toward, to bend the knee, to kneel before, to prostrate oneself." It is used to describe outward acts and inward attitudes of the heart. The focus is on the object of worship (John 9:38; Rev. 22:8,9).

Latreuo refers to a priestly sacrifice (Phil. 3:3), an offering (Heb. 10:2), or doing a service. It is demonstrated by presenting our bodies as living sacrifices to God (Rom. 12:1,2), being sensitive to the needs of the weak brothers (Rom. 14:18), sharing the gospel with the Gentiles so that they become an offering to God (Rom. 15:16), or meeting the physical needs of a brother in Christ (Phil. 4:18). When we serve others, we give a fragrant offering to the Lord as well (Gal. 6:10).

Hebrews 13:15,16 sums up the dual nature of worship well: **"Through Jesus, therefore, let us continually offer to God a sacrifice of praise—the fruit of lips that confess his name** [theocentric worship]. **And do not forget to do good and to share with others, for with such sacrifices God is pleased"** [anthropocentric worship].

Both kinds of worship are pleasing to God, and both can be exercised in the Sunday morning assembly.

What Conclusions Can We Draw, Then?

Balance is needed. Human needs are to be considered in the morning assembly. In fact, perhaps the greatest reason that we gather as a corporate body Is to encourage one another (Heb. 10:24,25). However, we must also focus on Christ (Heb. 12:2). So it seems that the answer to the question is that all three directions are to be considered each week in the assembly: upward, outward, and inward. The three foci become as it were a three-legged stool, and each leg is essential for the stool to stand.

Many Christian churches have been careful to restore certain God-centered elements to their assemblies, the Lord's Supper chief among them. Many have also been careful to equip the saints in Bible classes and sermon. Most have inherited an evangelical slant on their assemblies, and include invitations and baptisms on Sunday mornings. Is that enough balance, or can we fine-tune our assembly in other, more subtle ways, to help bring consistency in every aspect of our services, from usher training to styles of music?

Let me give you a brief list for checking on your consistency for your church. If you wish to be primarily God-centered in your assembly, then how does your prelude time focus on God? How much Scripture is read aloud? How do you think God views the "greeting time" at your church? How do you handle the sudden focus on people at the invitation time? What do you do about announcements?

If you have chosen to focus most on Christians, then how much time is spent focusing on the unchurched? How deep is the teaching/preaching time, and who is the focus? What kinds of songs are used, in what style of music? Are people encouraged to bring unchurched friends to the assembly?

If your choice is evangelism, then how do the elements of the service contribute to making converts? Do you celebrate the Lord's Table? If so, are the unchurched invited to partake also? If not, what are they encouraged to do during that time? How effective do you think the congregational singing is at convincing the unrepentant? Does your bulletin contain any terms unfamiliar to the totally unchurched person?

All of these questions are not to imply that there is any "right" or "wrong" solution. Asking what your primary focus is, however, will point to how you approach every element of the assembly. We should have a reason for every event, or we will eventually just do whatever follows the path of least resistance, or copy another church, patching together different ideas willy-nilly until the whole thing is a lukewarm mush.

None of the foci of the assembly is better than the others, as long as worship is done with the motive of glorifying God and being true to Scripture. They each have hidden dangers: God-centered worship may have a weakness in that it largely comes from the development of church traditions and not inherently from Scripture. On the other hand, the great weakness of an outreach orientation is a tendency to drift into pragmatic humanism. And focusing on the saints can lead to a selfish, ingrown, insulated church, which fails to please God or to reach man.

Each generation must grapple with the issue of pleasing God and accommodating people. Each congregation must work to focus on Christ and at the same time meet the needs of contemporary culture. If we all look to the Scriptures instead of running ahead and responding to our own instinctive or emotional reactions, then we will find unity in our diversity. Let me challenge each church to discuss a philosophical balance today. Who is your Sunday morning service focused on?

Making Hard Choices

Now we come to the place where you make those hard choices for your church. It is important that our churches have balance in their overall programming among worship, evangelism, and edification; but not all assemblies are a duplication of each other. So how will your church divide its priorities in each meeting? Which gatherings specialize in which areas? Churches through the years have made quite different choices in what they emphasize in their meetings, and yet they have successfully maintained an overall balance in the life of the church. Let's explore some models, and then have you make some hard choices for your own church.

The Model of the Early Church

As was discussed earlier, the major emphasis of the New Testament assembly was building up the believers while not offending the pre-believers. At least some of the early congregations had two separate assemblies every Lord's Day. Sunday was a working day in that culture, so they gathered before sunrise for the liturgy of the Word, a more public gathering dedicated to Scripture reading, singing, and a message. Then, after work, the faithful would gather again for an evening *agape* meal, which included taking the Lord's Supper. Later, the Roman government outlawed the agape meals, so the two services were merged into one.

In the postapostolic church, as the liturgy became more developed, they used easy-to-learn responsorial psalms in the *Synaxis*,[11] but longer antiphonal psalms in the Eucharistic assembly of the faithful. In the morning *Synaxis*, seekers could come and hear the Word clearly explained, and even participate in easy-to-learn responses, but they were not asked to pray, and they were not invited to take of the mysteries. If we were to make a chart of the balance of focus in the early church, it might look something like this:

THE EARLY CHURCH MODEL			
	GOD (worship)	BELIEVERS (edification)	PRE-BELIEVERS (evangelism)
Sunday morning *Synaxis*:	30%	**40%**	30%
Sunday evening *Agape meal*:	20%	**70%**	10%
Sunday evening *Eucharist*:	**80%**	20%	0%
Gospel sharing opportunities:	0%	0%	**100%**
TOTALS:	*130*	*130*	*140*

THE MODEL OF THE TRADITIONAL EVANGELICAL CHURCH

Most evangelical churches a century ago considered Sunday morning to be clearly for God. The music was stately, the rituals faithful, the words antiquated. Sunday evenings, however, were clearly for evangelism. Gospel songs were sung, with believers singing their testimonies and in the last stanza admonishing the sinners to hear the call; sermons were geared toward evangelism, with extended invitations and revival atmosphere. Wednesday evenings were prayer meetings, set apart for building up believers in study and honoring the Lord with extended prayer time. You might chart their balance something like this:

TRADITIONAL EVANGELICAL MODEL			
	GOD (worship)	BELIEVERS (edification)	PRE-BELIEVERS (evangelism)
Sunday morning:	**70%**	20%	10%
Sunday school:	10%	**70%**	20%
Sunday evening:	20%	10%	**70%**
Wednesday evening:	**50%**	**50%**	0%
TOTALS	*150*	*150*	*100*

THE MODEL OF THE SEEKER CHURCH

Willow Creek Community Church in South Barrington, IL, on the other hand, has made very different choices which are just as balanced. Weekends are purposeful seeker events. Everything is aimed at the unchurched seeker. The mid-week gathering has extended time for congregational singing, and attention is more focused on God and instructing believers. When they take the Lord's Supper, it is served in this mid-week gathering dedicated to worship. Small groups are dedicated to maturing believers and to give them time for genuine fellowship and service. When considered together, the programming at Willow Creek is balanced, but it is not the traditional choice of many traditional evangelical churches. Their chart might be drawn like this:

THE WILLOW CREEK MODEL			
	GOD (worship)	BELIEVERS (edification)	PRE-BELIEVERS (evangelism)
Sunday morning:	20%	10%	**70%**
Midweek gathering:	**50%**	**40%**	10%
Small groups:	30%	**50%**	20%
TOTALS:	*100*	*100*	*100*

THE MODEL OF THE EDIFICATION CHURCH

Still other churches have made the choice that Sunday morning is primarily to edify the believers. They might specialize in sharing testimonies and/or in in-depth expository preaching. Evangelism mostly takes place through small group evangelistic studies, through support groups, or through special seminars held at the church on Saturdays or evenings. Such a church might look like this on a chart (next page):

THE EDIFICATION MODEL			
	GOD (worship)	BELIEVERS (edification)	PRE-BELIEVERS (evangelism)
Sunday morning:	30%	**60%**	10%
Prayer groups:	**60%**	30%	10%
Outreach events:	10%	10%	**80%**
TOTALS:	*100*	*100*	*100*

The No-Choice Model

Every church needs balance between worship, evangelism, and edification, but not in every assembly. Hard choices need to be made for each program, as to its goal or focus. There is not really a right or wrong decision for your church's programming, unless you decide to avoid the hard decisions altogether. When you decide to emphasize one area, you must of necessity de-emphasize the others. It's hard to say "no" to an essential balance, which is why I call it a hard choice. On the other hand, if you try to chase all three rabbits in every gathering, you may fail to catch any of them. So, while the following chart could indicate a well-balanced church, I would consider it a *weak* way to achieve balance:

THE NO-CHOICE MODEL			
	GOD (worship)	BELIEVERS (edification)	PRE-BELIEVERS (evangelism)
Sunday morning:	33%	33%	33%
Sunday school:	33%	33%	33%
Sunday evening:	33%	33%	33%
Wednesday evening:	33%	33%	33%
Small groups:	33%	33%	33%
Other:	33%	33%	33%
TOTALS:	*198*	*198*	*198*

Most churches I have seen *think* that they have made a choice, because they have a different *style* for their different assemblies. Maybe Sunday morning is more traditional, and Wednesday evening they have a "Celebration Service" with more contemporary choruses and an informal atmosphere. Or perhaps they have targeted services, one contemporary and the other traditional. But don't be deceived by style. The deeper question is: to whom are the various services directed? Are you somehow providing for the true edification of the saints somewhere? Are you focused on corporate worship of the Living God at least once each week? Are you reaching out on a regular basis with the Good News about Jesus Christ to those who have not heard it before? Or are all of your gatherings variations of each other, designed to keep peace among the factions in the church, but not intentionally different?

Worse yet, many churches become enamored with the seeker sensitive worship of the church down the street or across the country. They are impressed with numbers and growth. So they ask shallow questions and strike easy compromises and wind up simply watering down their worship service. There never is a time for the saints to go deep, because they are always aware of outreach. Like a family that always has guests in the house, they lose the sense of intimacy with one another, and they substitute numerical growth for spiritual growth. What they end up with is Worship Lite. Worship Lite can work, if somewhere there is also an opportunity for "Worship Rich." But three "lite" meals a week does not make a Christian mature.

THE MODEL OF YOUR CHURCH

So, now it is time to make your own hard choices. Have your eldership come to consensus on this difficult question, and your church will be well down the road to worship renewal. These are hard choices, but to not make them is to miss excellence in accomplishing the mission of the church.

Who is the service for, primarily? Make a check, or assign a percentage, based on the relative balance of emphasis in each program in your church. Then add up the totals and see if you have achieved a New Testament balance in your church's overall programming.

	GOD (worship)	BELIEVERS (edification)	PRE-BELIEVERS (evangelism)
Sunday morning:			
Sunday school:			
Sunday evening:			
Wednesday evening:			
Small groups:			
Other:			
TOTALS:			

NOTE: My numbers reflect:
  ❑ The way my church currently IS (reality)
  ❑ The way I would like to see my church become (idealism)

In the next chapter, we will continue to lay the foundation for choosing a direction to go with your church's assemblies. Then we will turn the corner and suggest some practical ways to approach worship leading for your church, whatever its style.

CHAPTER FOUR

HOW OTHERS HAVE TARGETED THEIR WORSHIP

LEARNING FROM OTHER WORSHIP TRADITIONS

As we survey the practices of the assembly throughout history, we find a surprising freedom and variety of worship choices. Each generation must discover how to make worship relevant for its own culture, so the more models we can see, the better we will be at making our own choices.

We might use the old brain teaser to illustrate: Below, you see four dots. Can you think of a way to *connect all four* dots with *only two* straight lines, but the lines don't cross?

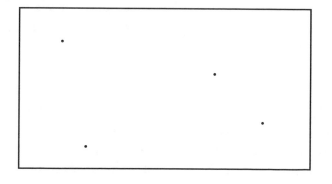

If you are not familiar with this particular brain teaser, you probably thought of several possibilities, but all of them either left out a dot, or else the lines crossed. However, if you thought *outside of the box*, suddenly the solution was clear! In fact, there are two possible solutions, if your lines go outside the box.¹ Churches have often been guilty of looking only to one another for insights of worship. For generations, we have thought *inside the box* about our worship. But there are examples in Scripture, throughout history, and in other traditions today that could give us fresh examples and help us to rethink our preconceptions. Let's talk about those preconceptions now. What follows are the common values of Christian churches and churches of Christ.

Traditional Restoration Patterns

For the next few pages I want to address so-called "Restoration Movement" churches directly.² Since this book is developed through a Restoration lens, some "insider talk" seems to be in order. However, many of the traits of RM churches are found in any independent evangelical American church, so general readers may also gain from a study of a representative subgroup.

The Restoration Movement seeks to restore the New Testament church in contemporary society. Most Christian churches or churches of Christ consider themselves to be a people "of the Book," and they look to the practice of the early church for their direction in worship practice, as well as in doctrine.

But have Christian churches restored the assemblies of the New Testament church? Historically, RM churches have been strikingly similar to one another in their meetings, their music, their language, and their buildings. Did they truly glean their worship practices from careful biblical study? Or, perhaps, have most of their worship practices come from copying one another? This chapter is dedicated to both a Bible study and to a survey of worship practices in other traditions to help foster fresh thinking about the practice of worship.

The assemblies in most of the congregations could be described in a few representative words: Christian churches' worship tends to be *Primitive, Conservative, Evangelical, Low Church, Isolationist, Pragmatic,* and *American.*

Restoration churches' worship is *Primitive,* in the sense that the churches consider themselves as "New Testament" churches. If a worship practice was found in the pages of the New Testament, especially if apostolic precedent seems to be implied, it is adopted as modern practice. But if worship practices were not present in the apostolic age, such practices are suspect at best. Hence, much attention is given to simple weekly celebration of the Lord's Supper, to preaching (as the rough equivalent to New Testament prophecy), and to baptism. In short, if a practice has scriptural authority, it is adopted, whether or not other denominations are doing so (weekly Lord's Table or disciple's baptism by immersion would be examples).

Worship in Christian churches also tends to be *Conservative,* in that the churches generally are Bible-oriented and theologically conservative. They also tend to be conservative in the sense of being emotionally reserved, and not given to extremes. The churches are generally not charismatic in doctrine or in personality.

Worship also tends to be *Evangelical.* For example, among some today, a church would be considered heretical if it did not have an invitation after the sermon. A service might have five or six prayers, but all but perhaps one is very short and spontaneous. Recently, "seeker-sensitive worship" has been a buzzword, and in some churches the "special music" has been expanded to two or more numbers, with emphasis on quality performance to present the gospel to the uninitiated.

Restoration Movement worship is also *Low Church.* The movement was born out of the early nineteenth century frontier revivals, and therefore takes on the cultural mood of simplicity and informality. The music style is (or was) the style of popular music of the era (camp meeting songs, then Sunday School songs and gospel hymns, then gospel songs); not the art music of the day (hymns, choral works, and other "disciplined" music). Churches tended not to require, and not particularly to trust, higher education in their ministerial staff. In worship practice, announcements are conversational, prayers are spontaneous, music is on a popular level, gospel songs are unquestioned, and buildings are functional.

The churches are autonomous, meaning that they do not rely on central placement or handed down policies to guide them. They have also tended to be *Isolationist*, in that they have eschewed cooperation with churches outside their brotherhood.[3] The posture of isolation has caused them to look to each other for their worship patterns, as well as their hermeneutic; therefore, up until the 1970s, most churches' assemblies were nearly identical. Even today, relatively few churches are looking to learn about worship from outside of the movement.

The churches also tend to be strongly *Pragmatic.* Smaller churches look to larger ones for ideas on how to grow, worship leaders go to "how-to" seminars for quick answers for their services, and all are asking questions about what will "work." What seems to be "working" for many is a switch to using a praise-and-worship format with contemporary music, packed into a one-hour service; or perhaps multiple targeted services to "reach" specific "audiences." Of course, the problem with being pragmatic is that pragmatists do not ask the question of what is *right*, only what seems to work in the short run.

Pragmatic evangelicals, then, create a brief seeker-sensitive service. Restoration Movement churches have been pragmatic evangelicals for the last few generations. The pragmatists of previous generations were seeker sensitive when they sang gospel songs like "Bringing in the Sheaves" or "Love Lifted Me," and preached an evangelistic sermon with "special music" before the evangelistic message and an invitation afterward. The current new generation of pragmatic evangelicals is also seeker sensitive when they sing contemporary choruses, and preach how-to felt-needs sermons with a dramatic sketch before and a nonconfrontational invitation after the message. The irony is this: suddenly, the last generation's pragmatists have begun judging the new generation as having compromised the ideal, or having left the "biblical" pattern of their own generation. Yet, the philosophy has not changed; only the methodology. What goes around comes around.

Christian churches are, by background and culture, thoroughly *American*.[4] The New Testament records the formation of the church in a Jewish and Greco-Roman culture; how does that translate to churches in America today? And how should we deconstruct and reconstruct from one situation to another, very different setting?

As in the old brain teaser, we may need to look outside our box for some fresh ideas of what the assembly could hold. In the next several pages, we will survey worship practice through history, to see how others have applied the biblical pattern for worship within their cultural context. Then, we will see what other groups today are doing in the assembly. Read with an open mind, and take notes as to what you might learn and can apply at your church.

ΠEW TESTAMENT SNAPSHOTS OF ASSEMBLIES

The New Testament does not describe the details of exactly what happened in the assemblies of the early church. If only the apostle Paul had simply written out an order of service, or printed a sample bulletin in one of his letters, it would be much easier to measure our own practice. If God had told us the texts to use and the style of music to sing, we would know how well we comply with His directions. But the Bible does not provide us with that kind of information. We don't have a bulletin from First Church of Christ of Jerusalem, or Antioch Christian Church.

We do have all the detail we need about doctrine and other matters that are essential, but we don't have an order of worship. But in the wisdom of the Holy Spirit, those details have been left out. Instead, we have much latitude in structuring our assemblies so that every generation in every culture can apply biblical principles to their own subculture.

We have not been left completely without guidance from the pages of the New Testament on this subject, however. Three snapshots in the pages of Scripture give us a glimpse, however brief it might be, of the life of the early church and of their assemblies.

Acts 2:42-47

The first snapshot of worship is found in Acts 2:42-47. It is not a description of the assembly, but a picture of the life of the early church as they met every day in the temple courts and in homes. It does not tell us about their style of music, or about the order of events. We are simply told that they devoted themselves to four things: the apostles' teaching, the fellowship, the breaking of the loaf, and the prayers.

They were continuing steadfastly in *the apostles' doctrine* (διδαχή, *didachē*). The apostles were studying the Old Testament Scriptures and were teaching the good news as God the Spirit revealed it to them. They recalled the words and deeds of Jesus, and interpreted the workings of the Spirit within the church. Later they made the conscious decision not to allow themselves to be distracted from this ministry of prayer and the word of God (Acts 6:2,4). The church today also devotes itself to the apostles' teaching when believers teach and study scriptural principles. Within an assembly, the Scripture readings and the message might fit into the category of the apostles' doctrine, as would Sunday School or other Bible studies throughout the week.

They were also continuing steadfastly in *the fellowship* (κοινωνία, *koinōnia*). They were sincerely devoted to one another, especially to those believers who were in need (see Acts 4:34; Gal. 6:10). Being devoted to the fellowship has to do with giving generously to one another. In fact, the same word is used to refer to the offering in 2 Corinthians 8:4; Hebrews 13:6; 1 Corinthians 16:1,2; Romans 15:26; and 2 Corinthians 9:13.

This passage describes their commitment to one another.

- ✔ They were *together* (they spent a large quantity of time in close proximity),

- ✔ they were *sharing all things in common* (what we sometimes call living in community),
- ✔ they were *selling their possessions and goods to meet others' needs*,
- ✔ they were *devoted* (the same word is used here as "continuing steadfastly" in verse 42) to these things:
    - ✝ to meeting daily in the temple courts (large group assembly),
    - ✝ and to sharing meals in their homes (small informal groups).
- ✔ Terms that describe their early fellowship include
    - ☞ "with one mind" (unity),
    - ☞ "with gladness," and
    - ☞ "with sincere hearts."

The church today can devote itself to the fellowship by similarly being generous and devoted to one another.

They were also continuing steadfastly in *the breaking of the loaf.* In verse 46, Luke says that they were breaking bread from house to house, meaning that they were having meals in their homes. But here in verse 42 he says they were breaking *the* loaf, referring to the supper instituted by the Lord in Matthew 26:26-29; Mark 14:22-26; and Luke 22:19-20. This meal was a significant centerpiece to their assemblies because Jesus made it clear that He wanted them to keep remembering Him by it. So when they broke *the* loaf, they were meeting around *the* table, keeping *the* feast. Acts 20:7 seems to imply that the very purpose for meeting on the first day of the week was for the purpose of breaking bread. Today's church can also commit itself to making the supper a pillar around which its assemblies are fashioned.

Lastly, they were continuing steadfastly in *the prayers.* Again, notice the article included here: *the* prayers. This term may refer to the 19 prayers that were recited by rote every day in the synagogue. It seems that the early believers, being almost exclusively Jewish, had no qualms with continuing in Judaistic traditions of synagogue and temple. Moreover, they were devoted to prayer itself, to talking to God. In the apostles' doctrine, leaders spoke to the people on God's behalf; in the fellowship, the people focused on one another to God's glory; in the breaking of the loaf and especially in the prayers, the people communed with God. This is a goal of worship: to commune with God. The church today can give itself to many things, but if it is not given to prayer, it is incomplete. Jesus said His Father's house *"will be called a house of prayer"* (Matt. 21:13; from Isa. 56:7). Christians do more than just "go to" the gathering; they "pray" the gathering. In the New Testament, public worship was synonymous with corporate prayers.

Conclusions for Worship Leading from Acts 2

- Be devoted to the ***Word of God***, and its careful study and presentation. Read Scripture creatively, and trust that God's Word will do its work.
- Build into the assembly opportunities for ***fellowship***. Let people know what they are giving to, build places for communication and friendship into the meeting.
- Make ***the Table*** the centerpiece of the assembly. Don't just do the same thing every week and hope for different results; be proactive in creativity.
- Give priority to ***prayer***. Organize prayer warriors to pray before or during the assembly, and take significant time within the meeting for extended prayer.

James 2:2-4

The next brief snapshot of New Testament worship is found in James 2:1-13 (esp. v. 2-4). He begins by describing a scene in order to tell the church to stop showing favoritism. A few details are helpful within the passage.

For instance, James uses the word "assembly" (συναγωγή, transliterated "synagogue") to describe the meeting. Nowhere in the New Testament is the term "worship service" used. It is simply *the meeting* or *the gathering together* of the *called-out ones* (the "church"). Moreover, it was, in its earliest days, primarily a Jewish meeting. It is only natural that the word synagogue describes their meeting.

Notice another detail at the beginning of his teaching: Suppose someone comes into your assembly whom you don't know. Don't miss this subtle implication from James: We are to expect "visitors" to come into our meetings. This person is unknown to us; he may be a believer, and he may not. But the point here is that he was unexpected. It is very proper and right for the church today to be ready for unknown people.

Now we get to the center of his instruction: Suppose this unknown visitor is dressed very well, with a gold ring and fine clothes. Another visitor is evidently a poor man in shabby clothes. We give the apparently-wealthy man a good seat, while the poor man stands or sits on the floor. To put it in today's parlance, we see a young couple, looking sharp, carrying Bible in arm, driving a late model car. We immediately profile them, thinking to ourselves, "Here is a quality couple. They could really contribute. Probably already Christians, and very possibly tithers at that! Let's invite them out for dinner after church and try to sell them on our church. This could be what we've been praying for!"

A shabbily-dressed single man also brings a prejudiced response in us. We think, "Oh, he doesn't look like a Christian. If he is a believer, he's probably backslidden. In any case, he doesn't fit our image. He will probably be one of those high-maintenance people, needing financial help and counseling. I'll have to invest countless hours in him, and then he'll probably not last. I just don't have the energy to invest in another needy relationship." So he isn't invited out to eat after church. We didn't turn him away, we just didn't give him "the best seat" when he came.[5] Favoritism has been a problem since the beginning of the church, and we must still repent of bias of every kind.

Hear this clearly: It is a sin to favor some people over others. Jesus said that even sinners love those who will return their favors (Matthew 5:45-47). James's words should cut us to the heart, for most churches discriminate and do not even recognize it. Has your church fallen prey to evil motives because it is so intent on its goals of growth and progress? The upwardly mobile church is an abomination to the Lord!

The Rule of St. Benedict calls for radical hospitality to be offered to any strangers. The monks are taught to treat every visitor as if he or she were Jesus.[6] Now, **that** will transform the welcome of visitors to your church!

Conclusions for Worship Leading from James 2

✤ Be warm and open to all, ***without showing favoritism***. From the front, and behind the scenes, make sure everyone is welcomed as you would want to be welcomed.

✤ Be ***ready for unknown visitors***. Have ushers trained and hospitable. Have seating ready for all.

---

1 Corinthians 14

The clearest snapshot of the assembly is found in 1 Corinthians 14. Paul corrects the practice of the church in Corinth. But if we read between the lines, we can find several principles for healthy assemblies.

The first and most basic principle is this: the *purpose of the assembly is to edify the believers*. Prophecy is superior to tongues because prophecy will build up the church.[7] How shall we apply this factor in our assemblies? Evangelism and self-expressive worship each have their place, but when we gather, we must focus on strengthening believers and building up the church. When we preach, we preach primarily to believers, not to God or to seekers. When we pray or sing, we build up the saints. We testify to strengthen the church. Let everything be for the building up of the body.

The second principle is related to the first and comes from verse 15: when we sing or pray, we must *sing or pray with both spirit and understanding*. What does this mean? Let's explore it on two levels. On the first level, the phrase simply means to sing or pray with both emotion and mind. Some churches emphasize emotional expression in worship, but the mind is not engaged. Others are full of Christians "from the neck up," who never really feel the truths they sing or pray about. On another level, realize that worship is to be both spiritual and intellectual. John was "in the Spirit" on the Lord's Day. Offering our bodies as living sacrifices is a spiritual service of worship. We are to walk in the Spirit. These are similar concepts to singing "with the spirit" here in verse 15. But let us not only be spiritual worshipers; we must also have minds and understanding to accompany our spiritual worship; otherwise, we may have personal worship, but the others are not edified by our expressions.[8]

A third detail of Corinthian assemblies is found in verse 16, where Paul refers to the practice of saying *"Amen" to respond to someone's thanksgiving.* In fact, in the original language, there is an article *the* before "Amen." It seems to have been the regular practice of the early church to respond with "amen" in some organized fashion when someone shared a testimony. We may even dare to call that a ritual. In any case, the use of "amen" indicates some semispontaneous, organized response for the congregation beyond only singing.[9]

The fourth principle helps to balance the first. In verse 23, Paul says, "So if the whole church comes together and everyone speaks in tongues, and some who do not understand or some unbelievers come in (the Greek word is ἰδιῶται [*idiōtai*]—an "idiot," as far as tongues is concerned), will they not say that you are out of your mind?" Paul teaches that the church should be prepared for visitors who are not yet "churched" in language, culture, or understanding. So, while the church should focus on building up the Christians, they should also *be aware of how the unchurched first–time visitor sees and hears what happens.* Paul clarifies what James had hinted. He continues in verse 24 and 25, "But if an unbeliever or someone who does not understand comes in while everybody is prophesying, he will be convicted by all that he is a sinner and will be judged by all, and the secrets of his heart will be laid bare. So he will fall down and worship God, exclaiming, 'God is really among you!'" What a powerful image this provides of the assembly!

How could everyone in the church prophesy? Later in the same chapter, Paul says there should be only two or three prophets speaking, so he must not mean public speeches here. If prophecy is speaking forth the things of God, it could include testimonies, singing, and teaching as well as preaching. How powerful for a pre-believer to be bombarded by the glory of God, from the parking lot all the way to his seat and back to the car again, as everyone he met boasted of the goodness of the Lord in his or her life! Unhappily, quite often we talk about sports and weather and "safe" topics. But if everyone boasted in the Lord, that collective witness could result in great piquing of interest, as it did for the assembled crowd the day of Pentecost (Acts 2:11, "**We hear them declaring the wonders of God in our own tongues!**"). The secrets of his heart would be exposed, he would be convinced of his sin, and he would fall down and worship God.

The apostle may have had events in King Saul's life in mind when he wrote this passage. In 1 Samuel 10:5-7, Samuel anoints Saul and then tells him,

> you will meet a procession of prophets coming down from the high place with lyres, tambourines, flutes and harps being played before them, and they will be prophesying. The Spirit of the Lord will come upon you in power, and you will prophesy with them; and you will be changed into a different person.

Prophecy can greatly humble and affect a person! Later in Saul's life, even after he had turned away from God, he was still affected by prophecy. In 1 Samuel 19:20-24 Saul was trying to kill David,

> So he sent men to capture him. But when they saw Samuel standing there as their leader, the Spirit of God came upon Saul's men and they also prophesied. Saul was told about it, and he sent more men, and they prophesied too. Saul sent men a third time, and they also prophesied. Finally, he himself left . . . But the Spirit of God came even upon him, and he walked along prophesying until he came to Naioth. He stripped off his robes and also prophesied in Samuel's presence. He lay that way all that day and night. This is why people say, 'Is Saul also among the prophets?[10]

Congregational singing could also be considered a form of

prophecy. In fact, quite often music and prophecy are put togeth-er in the Old Testament.[11] Whether prophecy is considered a form of direct revelation, or is a more general term for proclamation of God's truth, music is an important vehicle or accompaniment for it. So if, during the congregational singing, everyone around this uninstructed person sang with conviction and joy, it would be a strong statement of the working of God.

Notice, also, that the *emphasis* in the assembly seems to be on prophecy, not on worship, whether singing or spoken prayer or rit-ual. Nonetheless, the end *result* is spontaneous worship, generated by the newly-convicted believer! We tend to want visitors to feel welcome. God's goal is for them to feel convicted.

Paul summarizes and makes application in verse 26, which says, **"What then shall we say, brothers? When you come together, every-one has a hymn, or a word of instruction, a revelation, a tongue, or an interpretation. All of these must be done for the strengthening of the church."** In the church in Corinth, perhaps they had many excesses and problems, but this was not one of them. *Paul encourages everyone to come with something to contribute.* You might say he lists five types of prophecy—psalm, teaching, revelation, tongue, and inter-pretation. They came to listen, and also to bring the word of God to one another in some way. Everybody came with something, and there was opportunity for them to share it.

The next principle for the assembly is in verse 29: *"Two or three prophets should speak,* **and the others should weigh carefully what is said."** How many prophets speak in most churches? If the sermon is the equivalent of a prophecy, we have one. But God requires a witness, so that at the mouth of two or three witnesses every matter should be established (Deuteronomy 17:6; 19:15; 2 Corinthians 13:1, etc.). Jesus sent out the apostles in pairs, and that seems to have been the common practice of the New Testament church. Here is a challenge for preaching ministers to consider: Would your church members say to any stranger that you have two or three "prophets" each week in your church? How commit-ted are you to having a plurality of spiritual leaders?[12] How can you encourage the sense of two or three prophecies in your weekly assembly? The question is not whether you *should* have multiple witnesses; the question is *how*. More on this in the next chapter.

The next principle is found in verses 33 and 40. Prophets should speak one at a time, because God is not a God of disorder, but of peace (v. 33), and *all things should be done in a fitting and orderly way*. Paul calls the Corinthian free-for-all sharing-and-praise time back to order. He says, in effect, "You need to quiet down and talk in order, instead of everyone talking at the same time. You're too crazy!"[13] This principle prevents a chaotic shouting match in our assemblies. Even in rather staid, sedentary churches, we might have an "open mike" from time to time. Far too often, the "wrong" ones seem to take the stand every week. It turns into "Christian karaoke" time and "Can you top this?" testimony season. So be careful how you open up the microphone. Have some tricks to keep someone from droning on too long, or espousing wrong doctrine. Prearranged testimonies, topical small-group sharing, or holding the microphone in an interview setting could be ways to keep the sharing from getting out of control.

The last principle from the Corinthian passage is in verses 34-36. Verse 34 states, "**As in all the congregations of the saints, *women should remain silent in the churches*.**" If we seek to be New Testament in our worship, we must consider this principle as well as the others. Take note that whatever problems of disorderliness might arise in the assembly, let it not come from the wives. They must be leaders in peaceable, submissive learning, not in controversial talking.

To underscore the entire chapter, and especially the final point, Paul reminds his readers in verse 37 that these insights are not just his own opinions; they are *from the Lord*. So, as we take seriously the model of New Testament patterns for our assembly, let us also recognize that what little we may have by way of example in the pages of Scripture is not negotiable. If the Bible says clearly what to do in the assembly, we must find a way to carry it out, even if it is not culturally popular. If it is not clear, then we are free to do whatever is culturally expedient. These principles are not just Paul's opinion on how to have a good church service; they are directives from God. Therefore, let us learn carefully from the snapshots of New Testament worship services.

It is a wild goose chase to try to recreate the worship style of the early church. We do not know details of the worship, and there were many variations of liturgy in the early church. Beyond that, the worship style of the early church would not and should not translate directly into our current culture. What little we know about New Testament worship must be culturally translated, with many other factors taken into consideration.

Conclusions for Worship Leading from 1 Corinthians 14

❧ Make sure the focus of the assembly is on **building up the saints**. Don't get distracted by entertainment, outreach, or rituals. Do what strengthens the church!

❧ Make sure **people understand what they sing**. Don't let them simply sing song after song after song if they do not understand what and why they are singing.

❧ Give the church **opportunities to respond**, especially with "amen" and with thanksgivings and testimonies.

❧ Always be aware of the **prebelieving visitor**. Avoid spiritual jargon, which makes no sense to him or her. Emphasize opportunities for people to speak the gospel!

❧ Provide ways for **every Christian to contribute in the assembly**. Trust that God is working in their lives, and that they may have some stories to share about it.

❧ Provide some means of **multiple witnesses** to the proclamation of the gospel, whether prepared or spontaneous. Don't function with only one prophet.

❧ Do everything in **decency and in order**. The assembly is not a riot, and it is not a free-for-all. Do not let it become too loose.

❧ **Women should not be the troublemakers** in the assembly. Keep them from taking over the agenda or the platform.

Reflection and Application of New Testament Snapshots

Realizing how vastly cultures differ, try to apply the New Testament snapshots to your church's assembly. Some of the details below are fixed and nonoptional. Others may be changed or rejected by our current society, though they may have been expedient for the first century. A few of these may be subject to strongly differing opinion. This is an exercise in understanding our boundaries within the New Testament church. See how you do:

For each action, determine whether the decision is **fixed** (given, nonnegotiable) or **flexible** (can be changed, according to culture and opinion).

THE APOSTLES' DOCTRINE   A. Fixed   B. Flexible

1. How many men teach or preach.
2. Whether women may teach men in the assembly.
3. The style of preaching or teaching.
4. Length of lesson or message.
5. Whether and what curriculum is used.
6. Covering the whole counsel of God.
7. The public reading of Scripture.
8. Age-segregated (or affinity) grouping of classes.
9. Using drama, visuals, video or other creative media.
10. Whether professional people or lay people teach.

THE FELLOWSHIP   A. Fixed   B. Flexible

1. Whether or not there is a greeting time during the assembly.
2. Whether people are silent or talking before the assembly begins.
3. That offerings are set aside each week for the assembly.
4. Having weekly potluck/pitch-in dinners.
5. Having a vital small group ministry in your church.
6. That people pray for one another, love one another, and are fully united.

7. That people remember the poor.
8. Whether trays are passed, or people drop money into a box at the back, or they parade to the front when they give.
9. Having a food or clothing pantry.
10. Offering coffee and bagels to encourage informal lingering chat.

THE BREAKING OF BREAD

A. Fixed   B. Flexible

1. Taking the Lord's Supper on the first day of the week.
2. Whether the feast is called The Table, Communion, the Lord's Supper, or the Eucharist.
3. Whether people come forward, go to tables, or pass trays.
4. Who distributes the elements.
5. Using leavened or unleavened bread.
6. Using one large loaf or many small ones.
7. Allowing prebaptized (e.g., children) to partake.
8. Remembering Jesus.
9. Proclaiming Jesus' death until He comes.
10. A solemn mood maintained.

THE PRAYERS

A. Fixed   B. Flexible

1. Using written or printed prayers.
2. Praying spontaneously.
3. How many prayers are offered in the assembly.
4. Who prays (men, women, children, elders, etc.).
5. How long the prayer lasts.
6. Small group or large group prayer.
7. That God's house would be known as a house of prayer.
8. Praying for kings and all those in authority.
9. Praying for one another.
10. What language or dialect the prayer is in.

Put the eight principles for a good assembly from 1 Corinthians 14 in order for your church, according to how well they are being done. Rank what your church does best first, and in order down to #8 being what your church is weakest in.

❏ Building up the saints

❏ Understanding what they sing

❏ Responding when they share

❏ Accommodating the newcomer

❏ Every Christian participates

❏ Teach with multiple prophets

❏ Do everything with decency and in order

❏ Women should not be troublemakers

HOW OTHER TRADITIONS HAVE TARGETED THEIR WORSHIP

We now turn to three worship traditions, in order to study how others have targeted their worship. For each, evangelicals follow some of their worship practices, and don't follow others. Evangelicals have purposely adopted some worship practices from another tradition, but many times they have been influenced unknowingly. Likewise, evangelicals have purposely rejected some worship practices, even though they have never experienced them and would sometimes benefit from using those ideas.

With each tradition of worship, we will describe and learn from the tradition, then create a chart summarizing what can be learned from that tradition, and what evangelicals would do well to reject from that tradition. The goal of this next section is to move everyone into the column of informed decision. You can choose how to respond to the information, but at least you will do so on purpose.

	INFORMED DECISIONS	UNINFORMED DECISIONS
BORROW	Purposely Borrowed *(learned it and we love it)*	Ignorantly influenced *(don't know why we do it)*
REJECT	Purposely rejected *(spurned it and glad of it)*	Missing a blessing *(might go if we knew it)*

Learning from Ancient Evangelicals (Historical Liturgy)

Many people are misled by the word "liturgy," thinking that it means formal or high church worship. Liturgical churches, they picture, have organs and stained glass windows and kneeling pads and choirs. While it is true that many liturgical churches are high churches, historical liturgy can be done in any given style of worship.

What Is a "Liturgy?"

Evangelicals often think of liturgists as "them," and try to stay as far away as possible. But "they" are the ancient evangelicals,[14] and "our" worship style goes back as early as we have records. The oldest extant records of what took place in the assembly show a surprising amount of liturgical worship. The first-century church was not afraid of icons, or of borrowing from the liturgy of the synagogue, which was very prescribed and liturgical, although rather informal compared to worship in the temple.

The word liturgy comes from the Greek word *leiturgia* (λει-τυργία), which we usually translate "worship." It is a compound word derived from two shorter words: *laos*, meaning people, and *ergon*, meaning work. So the meaning of the Greek word *leiturgia* is the work of the people, or a public service. The Romans used the term to refer to a person who took on political office, much as Americans refer to a statesman as a public servant, or the British might refer to a ministry or a Prime Minister. Evangelicals refer to the gathering as corporate or public worship, or to the order of worship. It would be just as easy to transliterate the Greek word and call it the liturgy. In some ways, using the word liturgy helps to clear up some of the confusion of terminology.[15] It's not so scary, after all.

Some liturgical denominations are Roman Catholic, Eastern Orthodox, Lutheran, Episcopal, Presbyterian, United Methodists, and many of the so-called mainline denominations.

Sanctifying Time

Liturgical worship, however, also implies a particular approach to worship structure. In this case, liturgical worship is distinguished from "free" worship, because it follows the church calendar, while free worship does not. In that sense, when evangelicals celebrate Easter or Christmas, they are being liturgical in their worship, and might as well refer to their assembly as the liturgy.

Many evangelical churches have a bad case of *liturgiphobia.* They see any adherence to the church calendar to be, well, theologically liberal. They fear that if they talk about Advent or Pentecost or especially Lent it will lead to any number of heretical abuses of truth. Their understanding is often that Roman Catholicism syncretized secular or pagan holidays, compromising with and absorbing those ungodly traditions in a vain effort to "Christianize" them.

Ironically, many modern evangelicals celebrate Mother's Day, Independence Day, Thanksgiving, and various other invented holidays, including Boy Scout Sunday, Graduation Sunday, and Friend Day. To an evangelical, it makes sense to use these opportunities as a touchstone to draw a crowd and reach new people. We trust ourselves that we are not liberal and have not sold out. The irony is that ancient evangelicals had identical reasoning. Moderns and ancients have both tried to sanctify secular holidays to reach their society. For some reason, the similarities are seldom noticed.

So let me make a case for sanctifying time through following the church calendar. Many Christians sanctify their daily time; they pray before meals, have daily devotions, and pray before going to bed. Most also sanctify their weekly schedule; church on Sunday morning, perhaps Sunday night, Wednesday night groups, and so forth. Why not also sanctify the yearly cycle? The church calendar was set by the ancient church to revolve around the life of Christ. Every year, believers are taken through the cycle of His birth, His life, His teachings, His death and resurrection, His appearances and ascension, and the foundation and life of the church. That is the message of the gospel reenacted year by year by year.

According to 1 Corinthians 15, the center of the gospel is the death, burial, and resurrection of Christ. We preach the gospel, we sing gospel songs, and we reenact it in baptism and the Lord's Supper. Why can't our worship itself be similarly centered? Unless we have improved on that gospel, maybe we should consider making it the center of our yearly planning.

Many free churches are just as bound by thoughtless tradition as they judge liturgical churches to be when they follow an unstudied rigid order of worship week after week. To be sure, there is a danger of heartless religion in the church calendar. But every worship leader also goes through dry times. In those dry times, it may be better to fall back on the deep and refined prayers and statements of the Book of Common Prayer, rather than to rely on tired clichés. Planning worship based on the book of common song pales in comparison.

Honoring the Word of God

Here is another lesson to learn from historical worship: liturgists give honor to reading the Word of God. Many evangelical churches read very little.[16] The great irony here is this: many evangelicals think liturgists are theologically liberal.

In nearly every liturgical tradition, there are two or three extensive readings, balanced to include a reading from the Old Testament, a reading from the epistles, and a reading from the Gospels. Each of those readings is at least 5-10 verses, if not a lengthier passage. Besides that, they sing or chant or read several complete Psalms. In the course of three years, they systematically cover essentially the entire Bible in their Sunday readings. This is far more systematic reading than is done in the assembly of most free churches.

A further irony is that many liturgical churches are, in fact, theologically liberal. They are committed to read the Bible out of tradition but not conviction. Here is **Worship Riddle Number One:** *Why do some churches read portions of Scripture and reason away its truth, while others who believe its truth don't read sections of it aloud?* Evangelicals can learn from liturgists to give honor to the Scriptures by extended public reading of the Bible in their assemblies.

CongregationaL Participation

Ancient worship involves the congregation in some significant ways. Many free churches feel like their members participate in the service because it is comparatively informal. Yet, in most evangelical churches, there is almost no congregational participation beyond congregational singing. In the liturgical tradition, on the other hand, there are multiple opportunities for interaction and response, as the congregation recites prayers and interacts responsively with the celebrant.

Rather than passively listen to the leader talk, worshipers in the liturgical tradition enter into dialogue with the celebrant:"And also with you,""Thanks be to God,""Glory be to You, O Christ." Rather than passively sit and pray, these respondents kneel or stand and cross themselves, as they intone,"Lord, hear our prayer," "Our Father, which art in heaven . . . ,""Lord, have mercy." Rather than sit passively while communion trays are passed to them, worshipers in the high church walk forward and perhaps kneel to receive the Eucharist. Words are exchanged and eye contact made when they receive the elements. In dozens of small ways, the practice of liturgists is more participative.

Worship Riddle Number Two, paraphrased from Allen and Borror:[17] *Why do high churches kneel, low churches dance, and those in between do neither; they just sit and sing to their shoes?*

Again, there is a down side to much of that participation, for it is learned by rote from childhood, and involves the exact same words and actions week after week, year after year. The challenge for modern evangelicals is to find ways to participate and still be fresh and spontaneous, so as to pray with the spirit and the understanding.

REδISCOVERInG tHE ΠYStERiE8

The final suggestion of what evangelicals can learn from historical liturgy is the sense of mystery in worship. The Bible says that the relationship of a husband and wife is a mystery representing Christ and the church. Jesus said that the bread of His Supper is His body, and in a mysterious sense, it is. The Bible says that baptism saves us, and that it washes away our sins. Somehow, these are mysteries that work only in the mind of God.

The Greek word is *mustērion* (μυστήριον), and the Latin translation is *sacramentum*. Whether we call it a sacrament or a mystery, it serves as a symbol, a type, or a picture of heavenly truth. Liturgical worship is full of symbol, of mystery, and of the arts. Evangelicals in the postmodern era would do well to rediscover such windows into heaven, as the orthodox call their icons.

Ancient evangelicals had no qualms with decorating their worship space to sanctify it. In the catacombs, there are many icons of Jesus, of saints, of worshipers praying, and of the Holy Names. Art was considered a means of tapping into the mysteries. Liturgists today make much use of space, of light, of colors, of incense and smoke, of pageantry and processions, of festooning and reenactment. Especially in the orthodox churches, they proclaim the mysteries without need of explanation. They have layers of concurrent prayers and song and sounds and sights bombarding the senses and defying a full grasp in one sitting.

God Himself seems to have had no problems with certain craftsmanship and art, despite His clear commands against idolatry. He had the artisans create cherubs and pomegranates and use colors and precious stones and metals, and the Lord even gave recipes for special perfume and incense to be used in His worship.

Evangelicals have generally come from an iconoclastic background, and they tend to eschew anything that seems to hint of making idols. However, during the sixteenth century, many of the radical reform groups went overboard with their distrust of the arts. Perhaps it is time for evangelicals to revisit the creative use of the abstract arts to represent greater truths. As with other areas, this will be a challenge. But the days of rational explanation and logical study are past for American society as a whole. And so, modern evangelicals can learn from their historical heritage by using the arts and portraying and celebrating the mysteries once again.

What is good?	What to avoid.
Sanctifying time	Thoughtless ritual
Honoring the Word of God	Wrong application, or no study
Congregational participation	Insincere participation
Rediscovering the mysteries	Idolatry
Good doctrine in written prayers	Wrong doctrine
Doctrine of worship	Much taken from the Old Testament

Learning from Spirit-filled Evangelicals (Praise-and-Worship Tradition)

The Praise-and-Worship tradition crosses theological and denominational lines. P&W actually describes an approach to worship, implying, but not limited to, a systematic theology. *Praise* might be described as exuberant and celebrative, focusing on God's great acts. *Worship* is more intimate and reflective, and is marked by consecration and love. We enter into His gates with praise; we eventually come to the holy place in worship. So "Praise-and-Worship" is the description of the liturgical structure, and it is the unspoken structure of the assembly.

The source of the Praise-and-Worship tradition is the charismatic community, but today many noncharismatic churches also use the model. Within the last century, there have been four identifiable "waves" of the Spirit. The first wave took place around the turn of the twentieth century in *Pentecostal* churches.[18] They tend to be conservative, low church, and of southern culture, with a strong pastor and use of gospel songs in their assembly. Of course, one model for Pentecostal worship would come from Acts 2 (the Day of Pentecost), in which the presence of God was supernaturally manifest in the speaking in tongues of the disciples (hence, the name "Pentecostal"). Here is the model: a ten-day prayer meeting at which the powerful manifestation of the Spirit is evidenced, resulting in glory to God and the conversion of many.

The second wave was of the *charismatic* movement of the '60s.[19] There, the emphasis was more on a mysterious Presence, felt but not seen. Worshipers would gather and experience a manifestation during group open worship, or during prayer and ministry times. The third wave came in the '80s, and was led by Vineyard churches.[20] In these churches, music set the mood in which The Presence could be felt and gifts released. The fourth wave seems to be a more spontaneous intervention, almost taking a church by surprise.[21]

There are charismatics in every denomination, of every doctrinal persuasion. You might say the new ecumenism is based on common experience with the sign gifts.[22] There are several charismatic music publishers, largely marked by the propensity of praise and worship choruses in their catalog.[23] Charismatic theology is prevalent in many of today's popular choruses, but sometimes it is difficult to identify it at a glance. It might be hinted at in a song with an emphasis on the Spirit, on experience, and on power, renewal, or revival.

Some evangelicals strongly hold that charismatic gifts have ceased after the apostles, yet they buy and sing songs written by charismatics. It has been said that the songbook is the common man's theology book. If that's the case, Cessationists may put up a good argument in the classroom, but once the singing starts, everyone is a Charismatic. **Worship Riddle Number Three:** *How can we argue from the pulpit and yet share a common song?*

The Form of Praise-and-Worship

Worship planning in the P&W tradition is quite different than in liturgical or thematic traditions. It is simpler, in that it is not bound by church calendar or sermon topics. The worship sets are generated by whatever songs are "hot" for the leader or the group. The skill is in weaving the songs together skillfully to lead the congregation through authentic consecrated worship experiences. Participants start with celebration and telling God the things He's done, and move toward adoration, intimacy, and perhaps confession. They begin standing with their hands raised, perhaps dancing before the Lord (praise), and end prostrate before God (worship). Noncharismatic worship planners might follow the same pattern, but think in terms of tempo: start fast (rock songs) and end up slow (ballads).

Many of the pagan and religious traditions around the world open ceremonies with exuberant trance music, which opens them up to interaction with the spirits. Often the Christian praise tradition will do similar things. The opening two songs might last twenty minutes or more, with long extensions of instrumental work or exhortations for the congregation to participate fully. Some of those who are of the more reserved Christian worship traditions would be put off by such emotional frenzy, which might seem manipulative to them. But such is the nature of the praise tradition; dignity is gone, pride is brought low, and the believers willingly submit to being fools for Christ.

The assemblies seem to be based more on the Corinthian model than Pentecost. Songs are marked by simplicity, and in recent years the trend is for song leaders to say very little between songs in order to protect freedom for worshipers to follow as the Spirit leads. There are periods of time for personal and corporate prayer, repentance, healing, and other ministry. Usually times are inserted for admonitions from the pastor or a guest pastor, or testimonies and prophecy, or for exercise of gifts of compassion, touch, prayer, healing, or tongues.

A message is presented informally, but in Pentecostal traditions with much authority. At the end is an invitation to receive Christ and/or come forward for prayer. The congregation stands to pray (perhaps for those who have come forward) and sing (songs of adoration and victory), while those who feel led come forward to pray, to ask for prayer, or to lay hands on and pray for those who have come forward. This time might last a few minutes, and could go for hours. When this time of worship and ministry is closed out, usually some act of closure and dismissal takes place.

LEARNING FROM THE PRAISE TRADITION

What lessons can be learned from Pentecostal and charismatic churches? I'd like to suggest some major lessons for evangelicals.

Expressiveness. Many churches need to get over their *charisphobia,* and allow more personal testimonies, more body life, more lifting of hands and other worship postures, and more times of "free praise" where people spontaneously offer their individual expressions to the Lord in an organized yet passionate manner. Praise choruses are excellent tools for encouraging expressive praise. Charismatic believers come ready for active participation, with banners or flags or dance shoes. Their worship is like releasing a horse ready to run. They experience loud heart-cries and emotional (and physical) healing at the altar.

Patience. The opening song could last as long as an entire song service in many evangelical churches. The total assembly might last two hours or more. People come ready to interact with God, not just to be informed of some lesson; therefore, they are willing to stay until "it" happens, and then to tarry until "it" is over. Many time-conscious saints quench the Holy Spirit by not waiting patiently for Him.

The Holy Spirit. Charismatics allow for Spirit-led times of spontaneity, or times set aside for listening to God. They are not afraid to talk about Him or acknowledge any modern-day activity of His. They call for gifts that build up the Body by inviting testimonies, Scripture, and "insights" (sometimes calling them "words of revelation" or "prophecy"). Such actions are dangerous, for many believers could fall out of balance, but most clearly noncharismatic churches are out of balance the other way already.

Meeting needs. Pentecostal churches have altar calls, during which people pray for one another, confess their sins, or weep before the Lord. They anoint the sick, pray fervently for needs, and are often financially benevolent. Post-Enlightenment culture is hungry for a touch of the spiritual and experiential. This is no time for the Church, which has the Real Thing, to be afraid of it.

Hope. The culture and theology of Pentecostals puts great emphasis not only on the here-and-now, but also on the by-and-by. Many Black churches have shared that strong eschatological hope, as well.[24] If the future perfect looks better than the present imperfect, it is worth keeping before your eyes as you survive in a strange and alien land.

Mission and Interracial Unity. Worship Riddle Number Four: *Have you noticed how few conservative evangelical churches are doing inner–city work?* They may donate money, but most church planters and churches tend to follow the population and the money to the outer edges of the suburbs.[25] Likewise, most evangelical churches reach a single subculture, with very little ethnic or cultural blending. Charismatics have more of a tendency to go anywhere, to welcome all, and to reach multiple people groups.

Let me pursue the subject of interracial worship a bit more here. It has been said, with some truth, that eleven o'clock Sunday morning is the most segregated hour of the week. The "white male privilege" that many American Christians take for granted causes a huge blind spot. They *think* that they are open to Blacks or Hispanics, or to the deaf or women or any other group with less power. But they don't seek integration by changing their worship practices because they expect the rest of the world to come to them. Blacks will not come to White worship if they have to become White in order to be there. In contrast, the church in the New Testament was noticeably united across cultural and language barriers from the very first day. They found common ground in Christ, and their worship style seems to have adapted to include Jews and Gentiles, barbarians, slaves, and freemen.

Here are several aspects of Black culture, which also pertain to many other cultures and ethnic groups. They have much *emphasis on music,* and much blending of sacred and secular.[26] There is much emphasis on *interaction and participation* in music. It is not unusual for an organist to accompany the sermon through much of the message, nor for the congregation to dialogue with the messenger. The people are most often very physically as well as verbally involved in singing, preaching, and other events. Many European-Americans would see Black services as being, well, inefficient in their use of time. But Black culture tends to be *more event–oriented than clock–oriented.* Hence, assemblies will last two or more hours in most African-American churches, whatever the denomination. African-Americans and Charismatics tend to *celebrate truth,* while Whites and noncharismatics *study it.*

DANGERS OF THE PRAISE-AND-WORSHIP TRADITION

There are **dangers** in the Praise and Worship tradition. One is the *definition of worship.* The center of worship in many P&W churches is the experience of a visit from the Holy Spirit in the form of some manifestation. Many people come to the assembly looking to receive a fresh touch from the Holy Spirit, rather than coming to give to Him. It is fine to seek a blessing, and fine to convey your need for God, but when out of balance, it can become Christian hedonism[27] or narcissistic worship or spiritual selfishness.

Another danger is a backwards *definition of faith.* Because of regular visible manifestations of God's work and His blessing, many have *faith only when the sought–for manifestation has occurred* (faith in what is seen?). In contrast, New Testament visits from God seem not to have been manipulated or called down by the leadership; they were sent down by the Sovereign God, unexpected, and (apparently) unsought.[28]

A more heinous danger is that a naïve person, seeking some supernatural and spiritual activity, can be *susceptible to Satan's wiles,* including *demonic imitations of the Spirit's work.* The Deceiver can work miracles to deceive even the elect, if that were possible (*see* Matthew 24, Revelation 13, 1 Corinthians 11). It is necessary to discern spirits (*see* 1 John 4).

Lastly, many charismatic teachings have a largely *Old Testament doctrine of worship.* The New Testament has almost no record of tangible manifestations of the Presence of God.[29] The Old Testament is more physical, more posture-related, and more concrete. The Old Testament shows us examples of going up a mountain, burning up a sacrifice, falling prostrate, seeing smoke, conversing with an angel, seeing the glory of God. In the New Testament, there is very little record of direct conversations with God, or of physical acts of worship. Any Bible student needs to discern the difference between the Old Testament and the New Testament. This is a flaw in the worship theology of most charismatics that has gone unrecognized.

What is good?	What to avoid.
Expressiveness	Definition of worship
Patience	Definition of faith
The Holy Spirit	Susceptible to Satan's wiles
Meeting Needs	Old Testament doctrine of worship
Emphasis on future hope	
Mission and interracial unity	

LEARNING FROM PURPOSE-DRIVEN EVANGELICALS (THE SEEKER EVENT MODEL)

"Seeker-sensitive worship" has become a buzzword among evangelical churches in recent years. Churches such as Willow Creek Community Church in Illinois and Saddleback Valley Community Church in California are models for many churches desiring to be sensitive to the unchurched visitors among them.

More tightly defined, there are at least two or three levels of seeker sensitivity in a church's weekend assembly. Some churches try to be "visitor sensitive" by updating the music and explaining terms or events that occur in the assembly. The fundamental focus of their assembly is worship, but they try to make that worship as accessible as possible. Such a service is *seeker–sensitive worship* in the truest sense. Southeast Christian Church in Louisville might serve as an example.

The next level of seeker sensitivity would be a church that meets for both worship and evangelism. Scripture reading, prayer, the Lord's Supper, and other traditional "worship" elements still are an important part of the service, but music is somewhat more pre-sentational[30] than congregational, and drama, humor, video clips, storytelling, and message are coordinated to present the truth to those in attendance. A service built on this model might be better considered *seeker–driven worship*, as the needs of the seeker are given higher priority. Southland Christian Church in Lexington could be an example of this level of seeker sensitivity.

The highest level of seeker sensitivity is best called a *seeker event*, no longer limited by the goal of "worship." At Willow Creek, for example, the members have decided to inconvenience their own schedules for the sake of seekers. They come mid-week to study and "worship," so that on the weekends the gospel can be clearly presented. Sunday morning is the rough equivalent to an evangelistic service (harvest or revival series), which does not have worship as a particular stated goal. The weekend gatherings are almost exclusively presentational. Music, drama, and words are all used as part of a communication package to seekers.

THE BENEFITS OF SEEKER-SENSITIVE WORSHIP

What are the advantages of seeker-sensitive worship? Chapter two covered several of the concepts. First, it is *culturally relevant*. Sometimes we think we are worshiping the way God wants us to worship, but really we're just doing what works for those of us who are already saved. When we make decisions about the cultural package of our assembly, we should be making decisions based on those who are not yet there rather than addressing the needs and priorities of those who are already members.

Secondly, seeker-sensitive worship *obeys Jesus*. He said that if we love Him we would keep His commandments. One of those com-mandments is to go and make disciples of all nations. If we do not make disciples, are we obeying Jesus? No. We are sinning. When we purposely notice that there are guests among us, it increases our level of collective hospitality, and encourages us all to prophesy in order to win an unbeliever. Are disciple-making and hospitality acts of worship? Of course they are!

Third is simply this: *outward focus is healthy* for any body of people. When a church is not growing and dynamic, negativity and inflexibility tend to set in. Some folks want to freeze a particular tradition, others want to change it, and no one knows which choice to make or whose standards to follow. When we focus outside of ourselves, it protects us from selfish motivation in our value system. Why would we not want to bring someone with us to introduce him or her to the greatest thing in our lives? **Worship Riddle Number Five:** *When one beggar has found an unlimited supply of fresh bread, would he not go out of his way to tell another beggar where to find it?*

The Dangers of Seeker-Sensitive Worship

There are challenges in the decision to be seeker sensitive. A church can become driven by evangelism to the extent that *prayer, discipleship, and spiritual depth are ignored.* A common logical circle goes like this: the church exists to win the lost, who are won to join the church, which exists to win the lost. I would dare to assert that most church plants today are driven by this formula. What happened to worship?

For that matter, it is easy to focus on growth because of a *motivation of selfish ambition.* Growing a church is exciting and good for a career and an ego. So it's easy to get out of balance because of a blind spot in our motivation.

Furthermore, "common ground worship" can easily *deceive people about their status with God.* The emphasis in many churches has been on *seeker–inclusive worship*—worship that finds common ground between prebelievers and the faithful. We can all sing adoration to some nonspecified deity, and we can all sing love songs that reflect a common experience or emotion. People can come on weekends and get just enough of a scent of worship to mistakenly think they are true disciples. The worship feels good, and repentance is never mentioned. They are comfortable. Just like Laodicea.[31]

The church can become *driven by pragmatism*, adjusting its programs to what brings a crowd. If prebelievers set the agenda, including telling the speaker what topics he should address, is it still preaching? When the prophet is paid by the ones to whom he preaches, can he preach the whole counsel of God with integrity?

We run the danger of *"watered–down" worship*. **Worship Riddle Number Six:** *If a goal of worship is to enter the presence of God, then aren't "seeker–sensitive" and "worship" at cross–purposes?* No one can see God's face and live (*see* Exodus 33:20 and Revelation 1:17)! Our goal for the unchurched visitor should be that **"the secrets of his heart will be laid bare. So he will fall down and worship God"** (1 Corinthians 14:25). Having secrets exposed and falling down are pretty radical for a first-time visitor. But radical discipleship is the goal when we introduce others to the Lord of the Universe—isn't it?

It can be good to adjust our vocabulary to make the gospel easier to understand, but never to *change the gospel* itself. The cross is an offense, not a slogan. If our friends aren't yet ready for the "real" thing, we do not help them by giving them a polite rendition of it. These are questions to be wrestled with honestly and answered before adopting a more seeker-sensitive position on the Lord's Day.

Questions for Reflection

When does seeker-sensitive worship cease being worship, and become placebo or inoculation? If Sunday morning lacks prayer, the Lord's Supper, Scripture reading, and congregational participation, is it worship anymore? Can "the best worship show in town" actually be worship lite? Is it possible for worship to be what tickles ears, rather than what brings repentance?[32] Can worship have a form of godliness, but deny its power? At what point does worship become "Christian hedonism" or "narcissistic worship"? If Sundays change for the sake of the lost, when do the disciples get together for God's sake (literally)?

What is good?	What to avoid.
Culturally relevant	Prayer, discipleship, and spiritual depth are ignored
	Motivation of selfish ambition
Obeys Jesus	Deceive people about their status with God
Outward focus is healthy	Driven by pragmatism
	"Watered-down" worship
	Change the gospel

We have covered a lot of ground in four chapters, looking in depth at where we are and where we want to be. Hopefully, by this point, you have a pretty clear picture of what you want to accomplish in the assembly, including the congregational singing that we often call "worship time." Starting with the next chapter, we will look at different aspects of the assembly, and ask, "How do we get there?"

Reflection and Application for Learning from Other Traditions

List at least one strong advantage from each of the three worship traditions that you would like to see purposefully incorporated into your church's worship. Can you learn from or borrow from the advantages, without suffering from the weakness of that tradition?

1. From the Ancient Evangelicals:

2. From the Spirit-Filled Evangelicals:

3. From the Purpose-Driven Evangelicals:

PART THREE

Determining How to Get There

CHAPTER FIVE

Improving Our Worship Practices

Rethinking the Acts of the Assembly

Scripture leaves much room for flexibility in the assembly, and history provides many different traditions from which to choose in accomplishing authentic, creative worship. We have identified seven basic acts of the corporate assembly. How might we approach each of them from a more creative direction? Here is a tool to help rethink how we approach communion, evangelism, preaching, fellowship, congregational singing, prayer, and Scripture reading.

Resetting the Table

A Central Focus

In 1 Corinthians 11, we find that it was a high priority to the church of the New Testament to gather to break the Loaf together (Acts 2:42). The first day of the week is called the Lord's Day in Revelation 1, and the meal is called the Lord's Supper here in 1 Corinthians. Therefore, at many churches, when they gather on the first day of the week, they meet to break bread (see Acts 20:7).

Why was this simple meal so important to them? Among

other reasons, it was an activity that demonstrated unity and mutual respect for one another (vv. 17-22). Centrally, it was to promote the memory of Jesus, and it was a way to proclaim His death (vv. 23-26). Furthermore, the health and very life of some of the believers in Corinth were affected by whether or not they took the Supper rightly (vv. 27-32). Now, *that's* important!

In verse 24, it says that Jesus "had given thanks" for the bread that He broke. That word is *eucharistein,* from which the word Eucharist comes. In true Hebrew fashion, Jesus blessed the bread and the cup. The traditional words are something like, "Blessed are You, Lord God Almighty, who brings forth bread [the fruit of the vine] from the earth." And now as we take, may we give thanks, indeed.

Making It Special

Despite our rhetoric and our theology, however, in most churches the Lord's Table receives little creative attention. In some ways, less planning and attention goes into the Lord's Supper than into anything else in the service.

Many churches combat the lack of enthusiasm for the Table by celebrating it less frequently. But there is another solution: Make the Supper more memorable every week. If my relationship with my wife has gotten humdrum, and I can't remember our last memorable kiss, the best solution is not to kiss her less often, but to put some energy and creativity into my relationship with her. It is just so with The Feast. The danger, of course, is to substitute bizarreness or controversial novelty for creativity, so that the Supper is offensive rather than stretching and memorable. Nonetheless, some stretching out of our comfort zones may be in order.

Here are some ideas to consider for improving your church's celebration of the Lord's Supper:

Suggestion #1: Lead into the Table Well.

Somewhere, a standard pseudo-liturgical pattern for leading into the Lord's Supper has developed in many churches. The pattern looks something like this:

Communion Hymn *(the men come forward during the last stanza)*
Communion Meditation *(given by a "lay" leader from the church)*
Communion Prayer *(a generation ago there were two prayers, one for each element, now only one for both elements)*
Passing of Trays *(men from the church have a set pattern they have learned)*
Serving Children's Workers *(one or more of the men takes the trays to others in the building)*
Return Trays to the Table *(sometimes they are brought out the back instead)*

For some reason, many churches have felt that a "Communion Hymn" is the only way to prepare for the Lord's Supper. Surprisingly, it has not always been so, nor do Baby Boomers or younger tend to respond well to such preset functional use of a hymn. The hymn is often emotionally solemn, and if any hymns are found to be in a minor mode, they will be communion hymns. In many churches, other music is thematically chosen, but the communion hymn seems to be something of a parenthetical insertion into the service, unrelated to the service as a whole or to the message of the sermon.

Instead, let me gently suggest some ideas to make the service flow, and to highlight the centrality of the Table.

1. Lead into the time around the Table by letting it serve as a natural outgrowth and action of the rest of the worship.
2. Perhaps the message could be wrapped up and segued right into the Supper.
3. Perhaps the singing, Scripture, and prayer time sets up a certain mood and topic that lend themselves well to the Feast.
4. Don't let Communion time be an awkward and unrelated parenthesis in the service, but integrate it into the center of the worship moment.

SUGGESTION #2: SPEAK WELL LEADING INTO COMMUNION.

The Communion Meditation is in many churches the only spoken message trusted to the "laity." Many of the meditations are devotionals, unrelated to the rest of the service, but somehow tied into the subject of the Lord's Table. Few truly explain the depth of meaning behind the symbolism of the Table, and many become an elder's opportunity for a five-minute sermonette.

While "communion meditations" are not found in the Scriptures, they can help people remember Christ as they partake of the Lord's Supper. They can help to make each communion time fresh and filled with new insight. Here are some suggestions I gave our elders once to help those meditations be as effective as possible:

Avoid lag time. Before the time, as we are still singing, come forward and be in place.

Keep it brief. A two-minute meditation is sufficient to present people with something significant to reflect on during the Lord's supper. Watch the body language of the congregation; they start to shuffle after 120 seconds. If you type out the entire meditation, it should fit on one side of a 5½ by 8½ sheet of paper.

Make one point. People don't need two or three new insights to prepare for communion; the purpose of the meditation is to give them one new thought to guide their own meditation. If it takes longer than two minutes to say something, it probably contains more than one subject. Cut it, and use the other insights next time.

Center on Christ. This is a holy time. While your own meditation can and should have personal remarks and illustrations to draw people in to your meditation, the focus that we must always come back to is the Christ Event: Jesus' birth, life, teachings, purpose, death, burial, resurrection, glory, return, the heart of the gospel. (See Hippolytus's communion service for an exemplary way to include all these elements in a brief prayer.)

Include Scripture. Again, personal remarks and illustrations are excellent to use, but we must come around to the Scriptures themselves, which point us back to Christ. Most weeks you would be reminding the people of the words of institution themselves: Matthew 26:26-29; Mark 14:22-25; Luke 22:17-20; 1 Corinthians 11:23-25

Speak clearly. This is your time to exercise definitive spiritual leadership. Remember, this time is for the people, and you have an important ministry to fulfill. Stand tall, make good eye contact, speak loudly and distinctly, just as if you knew what you were doing (even if you feel like you don't!).

Make prayer brief. Talk to God now, and genuinely ask Him to help the people commune with Him during their time of partaking. No need to preach another meditation during your prayer; you've already told people something to reflect on.

Explain to visitors. Many visitors, especially the unchurched, have no idea what is about to take place. Build in redundancy for their sake. Let them know each week some of the basics: the bread and cup represent Jesus' body and blood, how we will partake this week; if you are a believer, you are invited to partake, etc.

Suggestion #3: Vary Your Approach.

When the Lord's Supper is taken every week the same way, it can tend to become commonplace. So every week, something needs to happen to make the Feast fresh and creative. Every week do something new, within cultural and practical limits. Don't let yourself fall into a rut.

The prayers and passing of trays in most churches are not usually problems in and of themselves. But the faces of the servers so often reflect the "sameness" of the routine. This ten-minute block of time in the service does not serve as the high point; it is far too often quite the opposite. And the sad truth is it could be so different if the church would be willing to take the risk of creativity and extra planning.

SOME WAYS TO PARTAKE:

1. Pass the trays and partake as they arrive.
2. Pass the trays, hold, and take in unison.
3. Have people speak to each other as they pass the trays. ("The body of Christ," etc.)
4. Pass the trays, hold, and partake as you will.
5. People come to the table to partake on their own as they will.
6. Elders or cell leaders or heads of households serve those who come to them and also pray for their needs.

OPTIONS FOR THE BREAD AND CUP:

1. One loaf
2. Matzo crackers
3. Individual loaves
4. Home-baked (pie crust recipe)
5. One cup (with real wine instead of grape juice, as disinfectant)
6. One cup, dipping the bread into the cup (this is called intinction)
7. Disposable cups
8. Glass cups
9. Family or small group cups

SUGGESTION #4: PRAY SIGNIFICANTLY.

When you pray blessing the Loaf and Cup, think in advance about what you want to say. Spontaneous prayers seem more sincere, but there are really few original prayers if you think about it. Most prayers said off the top of one's head are filled with trite cliches that come from other spontaneous prayers. We can do better than that. Study theology: To whom are you talking, and what are you asking, exactly? Study history: What have the great liturgists of the past contributed to the body of knowledge and activity? Study Scripture: What does the Bible say about what is happening here? Think about what you say, and when you pray, your words will be more accurate, while they are still sincere and spontaneous.

As a model to get you started in this adventure of rich prayer and careful treatment of the Table, see these notes adapted from Hippolytus in *The Apostolic Tradition* (A.D. 215).[1] This is a very early prayer, its theology would not make most evangelicals uncomfortable, and it is carefully said. Notice how broadly it sweeps, and yet how succinctly it is worded.

Hippolytus's Communion Prayer

Bishop *(to people)*:	The Lord be with you.	1. Blessing
People *(respond)*:	**And with your spirit.**	
Bishop:	Lift up your hearts.	
People:	**We have them with the Lord.**	
Bishop:	Let us give thanks to the Lord.	
People:	**It is fitting and right.**	
Bishop *(praying)*:	We give thanks to You, O God, through Your beloved child Jesus Christ. You sent Him to us in these last times as Savior and Redeemer and Angel of your will.	2. Thanksgiving
	He is Your inseparable Word. You made all things through Him, and in Him You were well pleased.	3. Salvation history:
	You sent Him from heaven into the Virgin's womb; and, conceived in the womb, He was made flesh and was shown as Your Son, being born of the Holy Spirit and the Virgin.	a. incarnation
	He then carried out Your will and bought a holy people for You. He stretched out His hands to suffer, that He might release from suffering those who have believed in You.	b. death
	Then He was betrayed, but He voluntarily suffered, so that He would destroy death, and break the bonds of the devil, and tread down hell, and shine upon the righteous, and limit death's power, and show us the resurrection.	c. resurrection
	That night He took bread and gave thanks to You, saying, 'Take this and eat it; this is My body, given for you.'	4. Words of institution
	In the same way He took the cup, saying, 'This is My blood, which is shed for you; when you do this, you show that you remember Me.'	
	While we remember, then, Jesus' death and resurrection,	5. Remembrance

we offer to You the bread and the cup, giving You thanks because You have held us worthy to stand before You and minister to You.

6. Oblation

And we ask that You would send Your Holy Spirit upon this offering of Your holy Church. We ask that You would make us all one in You. We ask that the Holy Spirit would strengthen our faith in truth as we eat and drink of these holy things.

7. Invocation

And we will give You praise and glory through Your child Jesus Christ. Through Jesus glory and honor go to You—Father and Son and Holy Spirit—in Your holy Church, both now and throughout all ages.

8. Praise

THE LORD'S SUPPER

Have a brainstorming session and write down ten ideas to bring creative variety to the Lord's Supper in your assembly:

1.

2.

3.

4.

5.

6.

7.

8.

9.

10.

Effective Evangelism

Evangelical churches have long valued the importance of outreach, including in Sunday morning assemblies. As was seen in the last chapter, using Sunday mornings for major emphasis on evangelism is a relatively new concept, within the last 200 years, mostly in America. Apparently, a century or two ago, first-time visitors at church were sometimes convinced that very hour of the truth of the gospel and were moved to respond. By the time the 1980s had rolled around, however, "cold" evangelism had become much less effective. In fact, if we want to reach strangers with the gospel today, using the methods of past generations may actually be a good example of how **not** to reach the unchurched visitor.

How NOT to Offer an Invitation.

Let's imagine that you are an unchurched person, who has never heard the gospel before, and you visit your church for the first time. Let's imagine that the sermon was powerful and God's Spirit through His Word brought conviction. You want to turn to Christ right then.

Block #1: You notice that as the preacher starts his last story, all the church members start pulling hymnals out of the pew racks and routinely turn to the invitation hymn which they have "held in readiness." Most are gathering up their things and getting ready to leave. You say to yourself, *If I go forward now I will make people late for their dinner plans. Maybe I will just stay right here.* **Is it good logic to put the invitation at the end of the service so everyone is late if someone responds?** Regardless, you are willing to obey the Lord, and you overlook the behavior of those around you.

Block #2: You listen carefully as the preacher explains what to do. Come forward as we sing, he says. But then everyone stands, so that your path to the aisle is blocked. You think, *If I respond now, not only will I make that lady late to the buffet, but I have to ask her to* *move out of the way.* **Is it best to have people stand when you have close pews?** Nonetheless, you overcome your concern and you are relieved to find that she was quite willing to have you respond; she even smiled as you excused yourself.

Block #3: Now you walk self-consciously down to the front row, and the preacher shakes your hand and smiles, pointing you to a seat on the pew. You sit down in front of everyone and wonder what will come next. The preacher has been encouraged by your response, and he extends the invitation for one more stanza. As the congregation sings, a well-dressed young couple comes forward as well, and they are escorted to the pew on the other side of the aisle. After one more verse, and no one responding, the preacher says, "God bless you" to the congregation and has everyone sit down. They sit and watch the back of your head as the preacher whispers to you. You think, *It sure is quiet in here. I must be turning ten shades of red.* **Is it best to have a hundred people watch the awkward process of someone in a private conversation?** Still, you stay, because this is the only way to Christ that you know of.

Block #4: The preacher whispers, "Why have you come forward this morning?" You respond, "I have decided that I want to become a Christian and give my life to Jesus, like you said." Briefly he asks you another question or two, and you can tell that he is uncomfortable about something, as if he wants to ask you more questions, though you are not sure what they would be. You think, *I have some more questions myself, if there were time; but not here, in front of everyone.* **The public is no arena for counseling about something as important and life-changing as repentance and salvation.** Yet, here you are, hanging on and hoping it will get better.

Block #5: The preacher gives you a pen and a little sheet of paper to fill out while everyone watches you, and he (thankfully) turns his attention on the couple that has come forward to transfer their membership. You are so pumped with adrenaline, your hand is shaking while you are trying to write, but you are also half-paying attention to the couple he is now introducing to the congregation. He extends to them the right hand of Christian fellowship and has them say some things. You wonder, *Will I need to know some of those answers they are giving?* **Filling out a form is the last thing someone should be dealing with at a time like this.** Nevertheless, you dutifully do your best to remember your cell phone number and age.

Block #6: *Oh, no, not a public speech!* The moment you dreaded arrives, as he turns to you, smiles, and extends his hand to shake yours and help you stand up. He reads your paper, mispronouncing your name, and introduces you to the church. You now must face two of your greatest fears at once: standing in front of a group of strangers, and giving an extemporaneous speech. The preacher says, "Unchurched Joe has come forward today to give his life to Christ and to be immersed in Christian baptism." You're glad he worded that for you. Then he looks at you and invites you to say "the good confession" with him. You've never heard the good confession, but you hope you agree with it as it unfolds. Each phrase is broken into pieces, and you find that you did agree that Jesus is the Christ, the Son of the Living God. And, yes, you do want Him as your personal Lord and Savior. So that's it. **Confession without careful study is a dangerous risk.** What now?

Block #7: The preacher instructs you to head on back to a little changing room. Hopefully some man or woman goes back with you. But don't count on it. You enter the little room and see some white robes hanging in a closet, and are told to put one on and come out that other door. You need to hurry, because the whole congregation has put off lunch to wait for you. Maybe they sing a song or read Romans 6 while they wait, but you can't tell.

Now, excuse me while I tell you my own experience. When I was twelve, I responded to the invitation in a similar way. And as I stood in the office that served as a dressing room, I had no one to answer some extremely practical questions: *Should I leave my underwear on? Is this robe waterproof? When it gets wet, does it become see–through–ish? How high is that wall on the front edge of the baptistry?* Now, I won't tell you what I decided, except to say that I made the wrong decision that day.

You are thinking, *This is embarrassing. Maybe if I just slip out the back door, no one will notice.* **We should never leave someone alone at a time like this!**

Block #8: Anyway, now you come down into the baptismal water. The preacher says some more words, with a hand on your back and one in the air. Then, if he's thorough, he whispers some quick instructions about holding nose, holding hands, bending knees and the like. And then you go down. It isn't smooth. You slip and there is a moment of panic when he covers your nose and presses your face under. **We would do well to better prepare people and to give them options they are most comfortable with.**

Block #9: Despite all of these challenges, when you come up again, you are exhilarated at what has just happened, and glad you are clean before God at last. You feel like you are truly born again! You hug the preacher long and strong, and pat him on the back five times. You want to dance and shout and praise the Lord. In response to your coming up, the congregation sits sedately and sings a schmaltzy chorus from 1939. *That doesn't exactly match my sentiment, but it expresses some nice thoughts. Are they singing that song just for me?* **We should match the mood with the song.** All's well that ends well.

What's the point of doing this little exercise? It takes a lot of conviction to overcome all of those fears. Yes, it's true that if anyone denies Jesus in this life, he will be denied before the angels in heaven (Luke 12:8-10). However, most of the believers would not be willing to go through a similar ordeal on a weekly basis, and most of those particular acts are really not scriptural requirements. They are inherited from nineteenth-century culture. So, let us reconsider how we can most effectively carry out our goals for true evangelism.

There are many options.

1. **Counseling room** (trained counselors filter out those who are not yet ready for public dedication and clarify what is needed, or simply pray for those with needs).

2. **Cards to fill out** in the handouts (asking for someone to make arrangements with the seeker to tell him more, or requesting prayer).

3. **Mid-week baptisms,** with introductions on Sundays (nothing in Scripture or church history prior to 1800 says the norm for response to the gospel must be done in front of the church on Sunday morning. In fact, if we believe that immersion is the occasion of salvation, it is an inconsistent policy to have anyone wait even a few days to be baptized.).

4. **Small group or individual explanations of the gospel**, with invitations in those more private settings.

5. A public invitation may not be offered, but a nonpressure public explanation of the gospel, with the option that people can **speak with a trained believer** about the gospel.

6. **General response directed to all in attendance**, encouraging a natural response to the message (in other words, Christians who want to commit to a deeper walk respond together with those who are responding for the first time).

7. **Ministry and prayer time** for anyone wanting to do business with God in some way (in other traditions, this is termed an altar call).

8. Have **elders greet people** as they come forward, and **stay with them** through the entire initiation process.

Here is a word of clarification: There are good times for public offering of invitations. Peter, on the Day of Pentecost, spoke to the listeners **"with many other words . . . and he pleaded with them, 'Save yourselves from this corrupt generation'"** (Acts 2:40). The ideas presented here are not meant to suggest that public invitations to Christian discipleship are never appropriate. In fact, among young people some invitations are being responded to in more numbers than ever before. However, long emotional exhortations are sometimes not effective with some people and may not yield lasting results in some people who were finally, barely convinced to respond. "What you win them with, you win them to," goes the saying. And week after week, invitations that end a service with no response create a certain psychological "down" to the morning, as if we were fishing and came home without anything to show for our time.

Evangelistic Invitation

Think of ten effective ways to offer an invitation to accept Christ, or perhaps ten alternatives to a traditional public invitation.

1.

2.

3.

4.

5.

6.

7.

8.

9.

10.

A Challenge Regarding Preaching

I am not and never have been a preaching minister, with the responsibility of providing messages on a weekly basis (though my children might disagree). Not being a "regular" preacher, I suppose, could make me an "irregular" preacher. With that caveat said, let me try to organize my opinions about common preaching practice, and suggest some creative approaches that might work for some churches.

Is a Sermon Necessary?

Preaching is an essential part of worship.[2] Scripture as well as church history supports making a proclaimed message (the *kerygma*) a prominent element, perhaps even the most prominent element, of an assembly. On the Day of Pentecost, Peter stood up to clarify the sign from many speakers and to proclaim the Good News "with many words" (Acts 2:40). The apostles discerned and announced that their calling was the word and prayer (Acts 6:2). Paul reminds the Romans that people can't believe in what they haven't heard, and they can't hear without a preacher (Romans 10:14-17). He tells Timothy to preach the word and to do the work of an evangelist (2 Timothy 4:2). He says that God chose to save people through the "foolishness" of what was preached (thus presupposing a preacher; 1 Corinthians 1:21).[3] Jesus spent much of His public ministry preaching in synagogues and outdoors in natural amphitheaters. So, proclaiming truth has always been a high priority for God, and by all rights it should be an emphasized part of the weekly assembly.

Vary Style but Keep to the Word

Preaching can cover a broad spectrum of delivery style and prior preparation. It can be done spontaneously, with natural personality, wit, and insights coming in a stream-of-consciousness structure. Or, a message could be carefully researched and studied, written in manuscript, fastidiously edited, and memorized verbatim. The two approaches to preaching are worlds apart, yet they may sound very similar to the listener. No doubt, many of the New Testament preachers did more of the off-the-top-of-the-head, from-the-heart type of speaking than most Americans today would consider healthy. Peter on Pentecost, or Paul on Mars Hill, or Stephen before the Sanhedrin, or even Jesus in the synagogue, taught many parables in reply to a question or for a particular situation. Most of us like to be more prepared, and American audiences don't want to waste their time listening to a low-quality message that makes inefficient use of time. The act of preaching is proclamation of God's truth through human personality, and those personalities can be very different.

Now for some suggestions for preaching in today's churches from this Monday morning preacher. There is one thing that all good preaching should have in common: It must explain the Word of God to people. I fear that many pragmatic preachers today have fallen prey to the temptation to trust others' talents above God's Word. So they preach from the First Book of Lucado or Second Swindoll, or whatever latest popular author has blessed them. Many preachers spend more time in other books than the Best Book in their personal study, and it shows in their preaching. Rather than taking the simple approach of expository preaching (Read the text, explain the text, apply the text), they illustrate a sermon until the original text is lost all together. The joke is a little too close to home sometimes, "I have my sermon all done; now all I need is a text for it."

This was mentioned earlier, but I fear that much preaching also is falling prey to what I call "creeping liberalism." Creeping liberalism is the kind you use when you are preaching for a non-Christian's funeral; you believe in hell, but it's just not the time to talk about it right now. So you say some comforting words and make no commitment about a sensitive issue for the family. Many evangelical preachers are so concerned about the prebelievers in their midst that they simply leave out certain topics. Rather than presenting the whole counsel of God, they find common ground and spend their entire careers trying to make everyone happy. But take note: the role of the prophet has never been to say what the people ask him to say. The prophet's role is to speak what God has commanded, no more and no less.

THERE IS NO RIGHT LENGTH

How long should a message last? Many folks in the pew would tell you they've never heard a bad short sermon. But a certain amount of time is needed to cover much ground in the message. Some preachers trust the reading of the Word, and consider that they need only speak a short time to comment on it (in many liturgical churches, the homily lasts only 10 or 15 minutes). Others incorporate the reading into the message, and provide a thorough commentary, the message lasting 45-60 minutes each week (remember, at Pentecost Peter spoke "many words," and in Mileta, Paul spoke all night). Most American sermons seem to aim for 20-30 minutes, while preaching lasts for hours in many other cultures.

MULTIPLE SPEAKERS AND OTHER VARIATIONS

How many people speak?[4] There are no records of two-man tag-team messages in Scripture, but Jesus sent the apostles out in twos, Paul says that there should be two or three prophets in each assembly, and God calls for every matter to be established at the mouth of two or three witnesses. There must be ways to apply this principle of having a "witness" to the Word. This is a strong way to word the question, but *who do we think we are* to be the lone voice for God week after week that we should not need a witness to confirm our words? We could accomplish a witness through testimonies, or feedback and discussion time after the message,[5] or through multiple preaching. The Communion Meditation may have the equivalent to a prophetic word. Does your worship leader have a prophetic role?

There are likewise many ways to deliver a message. Drama, storytelling, songs, and video clips can enhance or replace traditional spoken sermons. Moving the sermon earlier or later in the assembly could highlight it in a new way. Changing the location of the preacher himself (down in front, on a stool, behind the pulpit) enhances variety and could create a more teachable moment. Breaking up the message with Scripture readings, testimonies, dramatic sketches, or songs could help people's ears to stay alert.

Sometimes preachers are so predictable in their tone of voice, length of sermon, and style of delivery that people are lulled into complacency (or sleep) by the sheer lack of variety.

Whom do you address in your message? Scripture implies that building up believers should be the normal primary purpose for the Sunday morning message. Do take care, however, to address every person present. Filter your thoughts through the lens of all ethnic groups, of unchurched guests, of singles, women, children, young adults, and the aged. We must take care not to offend, even as we uncompromisingly present the truth of God to a lost generation.

This may be a controversial question, but let me address it to preachers: Could it be that the true motivation for many in ministry to emphasize the sermon is not so much to honor God's Word, or even the *kerygma* of the Truth? Could it be, rather, that selfish egos may be involved, leading to the mistaken notion that my pulpit performance is the most important event of the week for our members? Many preachers need to hear that the spoken word is important, even essential, to the assembly, but that it is one of seven essential events. Bible colleges and seminaries need to be equipping ministers in all seven acts of public worship, not just one or two (preaching and evangelism).

These are but sketches of thoughts and advice on options for preaching. I must leave it to those who preach regularly to carry them out or decide if any of these ideas is practical.

IDEAS FOR PROCLAMATION MINISTRY

Dream about and write down ten ideas that would increase the creativity and/or effectiveness of preaching in your church.

1.

2.

3.

4.

5.

6.

7.

8.

9.

10.

Enriching Fellowship

What fellowship there was in that early church! (*See* Acts 2:42-47; 4:32-37.) They were of one heart and mind. They willingly gave up the idea of personal property for the sake of those who had needs among them. They shared everything they had (not just some food)! They even sold land and houses to let the apostles distribute the money to those who had need. No wonder the apostles had such a powerful witness and God's grace was so apparent among them! No wonder there was no needy Christian among them!

The Twenty-first and the First Century

How would the American church be today if we started to live like the Jerusalem church? We would all live on much less, and would have our homes open more. We would not contend over church budgets, because we would be giving generously as the need arose, rather than out of a predetermined amount. We would all live as world Christians, contributing vast amounts to worldwide evangelism and caring for the needs of the poor among us.

If we were as committed to fellowship as they were, we would also take full advantage of every open spot of time when we assemble to speak of the great acts of God. We would be more "real" with one another, and would laugh and weep and hug a lot more. Family units would invite one another over, and there would be few "single adults" living by themselves among us, for households would welcome long-term guests to function as members of their family. Let us bring that day of radical hospitality back today!

There are many areas of weakness in American churches, but perhaps none stands in more contrast to the church of the New Testament than fellowship. Somehow the concept of personal property, personal privacy, and personal space has gotten mixed up with the idea of freedom in our minds, and we live comparatively isolated, private lives. In most churches, there is little true "one another" ministry taking place.

The "one another" commands in the New Testament are clear: *pray for* one another, *encourage* one another, *admonish* one another, *love* one another, *confess your sins* to one another, and on and on goes the list. But often all we do is *greet* one another, then sit in pews and listen to a lesson, talk about the weather, and go back to our private fortresses, with little interaction (other than gossip) until the next meeting. That is a very different picture than we find in Acts 2 and Acts 4. The believers were staying together every day, eating meals together in their homes, selling and giving and considering nothing to be personal property any more if someone had a need.

The early church lived in community, and all that it implies. They were wrapped up in and dependent on one another. But in America, the church lives the same as the world does: as Billy Sprague points out, 84 homes have 84 lawn mowers. Something's wrong with that stewardship when we share so little. We are far too private and too proud; rather than confess our sins to one another, we become offended when someone suggests that we pray in pairs or join small groups. We have relegated the concept of "fellowship" to potluck meals and church picnics, or perhaps to shooting the breeze in the narthex or vestibule. There must be a better way!

A Better Way than the American Way

There is, in fact, a better way. We can return to the radical hospitality that is demonstrated by that early Jerusalem church.

Jesus said that the mark of His disciples is the love that we have for one another. That love is to go far beyond the love that people of the world have for one another. People in the world *return* love. They will continue to give out love as long as good things are coming back. But we are called to *offer* love, whether or not it comes back. Remember, Jesus gave His love away before we gave anything to Him. While we were still sinners, Christ died for the ungodly. This is the example of love to follow.

HOSPITALITY

The gift mentioned more than any other in the early church was hospitality. The word in the original language means a "lover of strangers." Jesus had a healing ministry in which He simply healed everyone who came to Him. He didn't seem to ask questions first about their faith status and didn't issue commands like, "I'll heal you today, but I want to see you in church next Sunday." One of the keys to revival in the American church today is to be that committed to purposeful acts of kindness in Jesus' name and to live vulnerable, generous lives with one another.

GIVING

Fellowship also has to do with giving money. The word for "fellowship" is the same word that is used for the "offering." Sometimes people give because, "We have to do our part to keep the lights on in this place," or "We use this money to support missions around the world." But let me suggest a different emphasis that seems to have been prevalent in the New Testament: When they offered their money, it was not just to pay for a building or for the programming and staff of a church organization. It was first an offering to God, and second, a sharing with one another (*see* 2 Corinthians 8, 9). Someone has gone so far as to define worship: "Worship is offering."

EXACTLY WHAT IS "FELLOWSHIP" ANYWAY?

Fellowship may take a radical new approach in our thinking. Fellowship is more than just two fellows in the same ship; it is shared lives on the deepest level. We often think of ourselves as individuals, rather than as a community. When we take the Lord's Supper with individual pieces of bread and individual cups, it may betray our ecclesiology. We see ourselves as a conglomerate of different people who happen to be members of the same church. In contrast, God calls us His *people*, not just His *persons*. We are *one* loaf, we drink from *one* cup, and we are all members of *one* body, not people with a common interest. We belong to one another, and the Lord calls us to reflect that unity in our lifestyles. There is no more Jew nor Greek, male nor female, slave nor free, as long as we are His.

We are also a royal priesthood. Some have said, "We are Protestants, so we don't have priests." Nothing could be further from the truth! We are *all* priests, not *none* of us! As such, we can hear confessions, serve communion, give blessings, and carry each other's burdens to God.

Many today think that the church is made up of people who have accepted Jesus as Savior and Lord. They may look just like the people of the "world" and may have the same taste in entertainment. They may listen to the same radio stations, read the same magazines, and have the same divorce rate (recent reports indicate that perhaps Christian divorce rates are even a little higher than in the world). In other words, many people think that Christians only differ from non-Christians in *what they believe*. But if we understand what the Bible says about who the church is, we would not make this mistake.

Consider briefly what the Bible says the church is:

The church (that's us!) is most commonly called the *ekklesia*, or the "called out assembly." Called out from what, you might wonder? The church is called the *Jerusalem above* (Gal. 4:26), and the *heavenly Jerusalem* (Heb. 12:22; Rev. 21:2). The church was called to *come out from* Babylon and be separate. The believers were called Christians (Acts 11:26), or Christ-followers; also followers of *the Way* (Acts 9:2, etc.), *the way of God* (Acts 18:26), and *the way of truth* (2 Pet. 2:2). New Testament writers often call other believers *the saints*, or the holy ones; those who belong to and share in the Holy One.

What's more, the church is a *body*, the *body of Christ* (1 Cor. 12:13; Eph. 4:4), a *flock* protected by its Shepherd, Jesus (Acts 20:28; 1 Pet. 5:2,3), or as *branches* of the vine, who is Christ (John 15:1-5). We are the *household of faith* (Gal. 6:10; Eph. 2:19), the *family of God*, in which He is the Father, and the *bride* of the Lamb Jesus (Rev. 19:7, etc.). What's more, we together are a *temple* of the Holy Spirit (1 Cor. 3:16,17; 2 Cor. 6:16), a *new creation* (2 Cor. 5:17), and the *kingdom of God* (Rom. 14:17; 1 Cor. 4:20; Col. 4:11; 2 Thess. 1:5).

What kind of pictures do those terms bring to mind?

➤ Does it sound like people whose only difference from the world is their set of beliefs?

➤ Does it sound like isolated rural suburbanites who live three miles from the nearest sin?

➤ Does it sound like people who are Jewish, Gentile, male, female, slave, and free?

➤ What image do you have of the church?

Let me help to refine it some more.

Initially, Christianity was an *urban movement*, starting in prominent cities and only later infiltrating to rural areas. They were not afraid to live next door to the world, nor to use their considerable spiritual influence and the power of God to affect those around them.

The church was also a *countercultural movement*. The worldview of the first generation of Christians was strongly at odds with both Jewish and Gentile/pagan paradigms. Consequently, these urban countercultures were said to have "turned the world upside down."

They were a *radical fellowship*, busying itself with the message of the King and quietly bringing about a cultural crusade that changed the history of the world.

What about us?

➤ Do we blend in with the world so much that the only difference between us and the world is our theology?

➤ Or, on the other hand, do we cling to protective isolation so that we make no impact on our worldly next-door neighbors?

➤ Or do we even get sidetracked by "family values" and other cultural issues so that we are "only" cultural conservatives, but not a radically different fellowship?

Here's an idea: Let's *be* the *CHURCH!* Let's be that fellowship of people who have been radically remade from the inside out, who live above the world and model a radically different lifestyle, and who boldly speak our faith to those who will hear our radical message. Let's start today!

Improving Our Fellowship/Sharing/Giving

Think about fellowship and one-another ministry at your church, and write down ten ideas for how to improve fellowship.

1.

2.

3.

4.

5.

6.

7.

8.

9.

10.

Congregational Singing

Why and What Should We Sing?

There are several things that can or should be accomplished

in our congregational singing. According to Ephesians 5:19 and Colossians 3:16, we are to sing for these reasons:

- **Teaching.** Our songs should be full of doctrine. We sing them to learn, to love what we learn, and to memorize and reflect on what we learn. Every song should be worthy by containing enough truth to be worth reflecting on it.
- **Admonishing.** Our songs should bring conviction. We may sing happy, celebratory songs together, but our material should also be of enough prophetic conviction that we can use them to bring about repentance in one another before the Lord.
- **Speaking to one another.** The act of singing is to be a community act, in which our unity is celebrated. Every song should represent the offering of the Body as a whole, singing the songs of the Church to the church. Note that every song need not be addressed directly to the Lord.
- **Psalms.** We need to sing from the Book of Psalms, or according to the pattern found in that book. (See the article below.)
- **Hymns.** We are to sing New Testament or newly composed canticles which tell of Christ and proclaim His praise. (See the article below.)
- **Spiritual songs.** We are to create new songs, which are spiritually-generated and spiritually-directed. These can be songs of testimony of the spiritual life, songs of prophecy from the Spirit, or even wordless songs of praise offered on the breath.
- **Giving thanks to God.** Ultimately, every song that the congregation sings is directed to the Lord with thanksgiving.

The assembly also gives room for testimonies (or prophecy) by individuals, so if that testimony happens to be set musically, it is perfectly appropriate to share. But note that there is no direct reference to presentation music in the assembly; the Bible does, however, talk about congregational singing. So at my church, we have decided that the primary choir is the congregational choir, and the balance of time must be given to honoring God with corporate singing, not presentation songs. Since initiating that change of balance, we have been blessed by some side benefits. The potential for egos getting out of control or of hurt feelings for being overlooked in the solo rotation is greatly diminished. Unity reigns, even in the music department! Each church must decide where to find its own balance between congregation and presentation, but for us right now, one song once or twice a month that has special significance to the morning seems to feel like the right balance.

ARE WE REALLY Singing the Psalms?

The Church has rediscovered the Book of Psalms! For years neglected by evangelicals, Psalms have reemerged from their long exile in the middle of our Bibles to find their place among hymns and spiritual songs once again. New Scripture choruses have been introduced into most of our churches, to the point that some churches are using them almost exclusively. So we are singing the Psalms now! But are we *really* singing the Psalms?

THE PROBLEM

Contemporary choruses have much that is good.[6] They are often, perhaps even usually, Scripture choruses, often taken from the Psalms, and this is extremely commendable. But what bothers me is that they seem to be taken from short, carefully selected sections of Psalms, geared only toward what is currently a "hot" subject. "Hot" subjects of the seventies seem to have been Testimony and Evangelism and the Names of God. In the eighties, charismatic worship added subjects of the Holy Spirit, the Royalty and Majesty of Jesus, and Signs and Wonders in His name. Hot topics of the nineties continued in the vein of Spiritual Warfare, and more recently the hottest topic is Personal Love Songs. The rich young Baby Boomer might say, "All these we have sung since our childhood. What do we still lack?"

André Resner, Jr. suggests that we have neglected the subject of Lament.[7] Almost half of the Psalms have either individual or community lament.[8] In contrast, no Christian hymnals today seem to have even a category in their topical indexes for Lament. Likewise, a few years ago I compared four evangelical hymnals to the Book of Psalms. I discovered that some of the evangelical hymnals of the 1970s had been badly neglecting the area of worship (especially individual prayer) as they focused on songs of testimony and invitation.[9] Believers were telling their story to unbelievers more than they were addressing the Lord. These may be some weaknesses in our hymnals, but that trend has largely passed.

But what about today's Psalm choruses? If previous evangelical hymnals were biased toward evangelistic testimony, and if they have neglected the concept of biblical lament, what about the choruses more recently in use? How do they actually stack up to the Book of Psalms itself? New Testament practice, church history, and many theologians and liturgists concur that the Psalms are the standard by which all congregational songs can and should be measured.[10]

A quick survey of Scripture sources for a modern collection reveals that about a third of them are drawn directly from the Book of Psalms. Unlike psalters of the past, however, which included every verse of every psalm, today's praise and worship choruses seem to choose very short, very select verses of Scripture. Are some topics being overlooked? Has the Christian community satisfied itself with the "form" of Scripture choruses but neglected the "substance" of the whole counsel of God?

THE CASE OF PSALMS V. CHORUSES

In this current age, the Book of Psalms may well sue contemporary Scripture choruses for misrepresentation. The accusation would be that Scripture choruses use the label "Psalms," but do not fairly represent the balance of what the Psalms contain. Called to represent the plaintiff are a 2002 CCLI Top 100 list and Word's collection of choruses *Songs for Praise and Worship*.

In 1 Chronicles 16:4 it says that David "appointed . . . Levites to minister before the ark of the LORD, to make petition, to give thanks, and to praise the Lord, the God of Israel." This verse seems to imply four purposes for the Levites (some of whom would be musicians): minister before the ark (*priestly songs*), make petition (*requesting songs*), give thanks (*thanksgiving songs*), and praise the Lord (*songs of worship and praise*). To this passage might be added 1 Chronicles 25:1, where some of the men are set apart "**for the ministry of prophesying, accompanied by harps, lyres and cymbals.**" So a fifth category of prophecy (*teaching and exhorting songs*) is added (see also Eph. 5:19; Col. 3:16). These five categories correspond roughly to the types of expression Artur Weiser suggests in his categorization of the Psalms.[11]

Presentation of the Evidence: The Book of Psalms.

Praise songs are found in most of the book of Psalms. *Thanksgiving* songs and *praise and worship* songs overlap, and are sometimes hard to distinguish from each other. The writer may be giving thanks to the Lord for things He has done and move indistinguishably into the realm of praise; or when elaborating on things he praises God for, the writer may also list some personal benefits. Altogether, thanksgiving, praise, and worship make up more than half of the verses in the book of Psalms.

Petition songs are much more common in the Psalms. Petitions are often individual lament before the Lord. Sometimes they are corporate or national lament. Some of the psalms are even imprecatory psalms (Ps. 35:1: "**Contend, O Lord, with those who contend with me**") or penitential psalms. More than a fourth of the words in the book of Psalms contain some form of petition, directly addressing God and asking Him for something. It is the second most common category in the canonical collection.

Many of the psalms are also *prophecy* songs. Prophecy songs will contain wisdom or didactic elements, some piece of doctrine or teaching or some call to repentance or other exhortation. Prophecy songs are directed toward people rather than toward God. Prophecy is a relatively rare category in the Book of Psalms.

Priestly songs are the smallest of the categories in the Psalms. They represent the relatively rare occurrences where the writer speaks of presenting sacrifices and offerings to God, or being in the presence of God and ministering to Him in some way. Most are quite brief, often just one verse that mentions bringing a sacrifice or lifting hands in the holy place. "Ministering to the LORD" in a self-referential fashion is relatively rare in the Book of Psalms.

Choruses and Psalms
Percentage of Total Categories

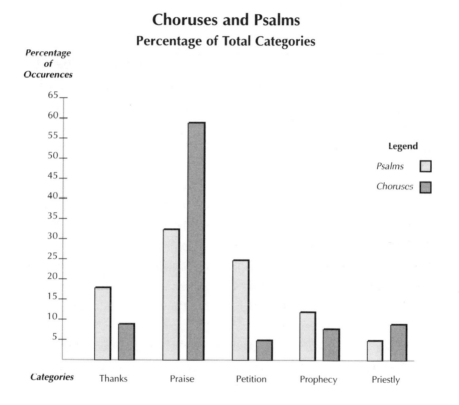

THE CHORUSES

The defense for modern choruses could point out that they reflect the balance of the Book of Psalms in many ways: Both choruses and Psalms have a strong emphasis on thanksgiving and praise and worship elements. Both are similar in the amount of priestly songs and prophecy songs. But there is almost a total lack of petition in the choruses. Most of these petitions ask God to help the worshiper love Him more or please Him, so they are personal priestly petitions. And almost none of those petitions contain any kind of lament. So while a sizeable number of the psalms contain some petition, less than ten percent of the choruses have any.

What do the choruses have instead of petition? Praise and worship. See the graph on the previous page comparing the choruses and the Psalms.

Final Arguments

Some of today's bias toward praise and worship is proper. This is, after all, the New Testament era. Christ has come and has fulfilled the prophecies. He has brought about mankind's forgiveness and spiritual healing. The promise of eternal life is secured, and the seal of the Holy Spirit has been granted. There is less need for dwelling in doubt or despair in light of all that we have in Christ. Rather, rejoicing in the promise of heaven or in the fulfilled hope of the Old Testament is in order. However, there does remain a sense in which the human body is not fully saved, and there does remain a sense of groaning for the completion of all things in Christ. The choruses would do well to reflect the full gospel of redemption in a fallen world. Of course, expressions other than singing happen in our assemblies, and they can (and do) contain some of these elements.

The Psalms are longer and less tightly organized than modern Scripture choruses.[12] In the process of choosing one verse from a given Psalm, it would be natural to choose the optimistic, rich core verse of praise from among the other verses.

The Decision of the Jury

What is the conclusion of the matter? The current return to Scripture choruses is positive. The use of brevity is necessary. The Church is gaining a good supply of praise and worship songs. But the Church could use more songs (and hymns) of petition. Let the Church give thanks to the Lord; let her honor her King; let her be built up with truth and have everyone prophesy in her midst. But let her also in prayer and petition, with thanksgiving, present her requests to God. And then the peace of God, which transcends all understanding, will guard her heart and her mind in Christ Jesus. Let's *really* sing the Psalms!

CONGREGATIONAL SINGING

Think of ten ways to improve the congregational singing at your church and record them here.

1.

2.

3.

4.

5.

6.

7.

8.

9.

10.

GIVING OURSELVES TO PRAYER

I fear that in trying to be seeker sensitive, one of the evangelical church's greatest compromises is prayer. Trying to shorten the assembly to 60 or 70 minutes and trying to keep the momentum going, we have limited our prayer to five or six very brief, token prayers, offered up with little forethought and even less zeal. There is a whole world to pray for, but in many of our churches the only thing we can think of is the hospital list and the public "worry" list. Of course, we should pray for the sick, and of course we must pray about public concerns. But what about the *rest* of the world? When it's time to pray, let's pray rather than play. God wants His house to be known as a house of prayer.

A friend of mine went to a Francis Schaeffer seminar several years ago. The seminar was two days long, and the first day not one prayer was offered up. My friend began to conclude that Schaeffer was too busy being a brilliant philosopher to the neglect of prayer. But on the second day, Schaeffer led the group in prayer, and it was powerful, sweeping, sincere, and more earnest than any my friend had experienced. He concluded that Schaeffer did not withhold from public prayer on the first day because he didn't think prayer important; rather, he thought prayer to be so important that short, token prayers paled in comparison. When it was time to pray, he *prayed!* Similarly, I recommend fewer, stronger prayers in an assembly, rather than shallow tokens. As Melody Green wrote in song some years ago, "Make my life a prayer to You. . . . no token prayers."

We need to realize that prayer is not something that we just enter into and come out of; it is a spiritual state of communion with the Lord, tantamount to walking in the Spirit. We must not take God for granted all week long, and then toss Him little phrases and cliches. David describes himself in Psalm 109:4 as being a man of prayer: "**I give myself unto prayer**" (KJV). Literally, that is translated, "I am prayer." How is *your* prayer life? Are you in constant contact with the Almighty, living in a running conversation with your Creator? Worship is 24 hours a day/7 days a week, prayer is 24/7, being filled with the Spirit is 24/7. I wonder if they are roughly synonymous? Is prayer worship? Perhaps it is the *highest* act of worship!

Most churches start with a spontaneous opening prayer, often called an invocation. In it, we just really thank the Lord for this day when we can come into His house, and blah blah. Later in the service, someone prays for communion, for the pastoral prayer, for offering, before and/or after the message, and as a benediction. At least two of those prayers often begin with the same sentence: "Lord, we just really thank you for the beautiful weather today, and for this day when we can freely come into your house and yada yada."

So, what can we do? We can bless the Lord! Seek His face! Mention the persecuted church! Pray for missionaries! Pray for lost souls! Pray for struggling marriages and rebellious children and confused saints and boldness in witness and financial needs and those who are sick or injured or friendless or homeless! Pray for the person next to you! Pray for the schools and the teachers and our children! Confess our sins to God! Pray for the seekers, by name! If we do not ask, we will not have (James 4:2)!

If you are in a public assembly and you have an opportunity to lead people in public prayer, here is some practical advice: **Talk to God** when you pray. This is not a time to preview or review your sermon, as if the most important thing that happens on Sunday morning is the lesson! It is not a time to give announcements in a subtle way. It is especially not time to gossip by adding some tidbit of harmful insider information about someone. Study theology and let your understanding of the Trinity and the authority and qualities of God saturate your prayer language. Study your Bible and let the example of New Testament prayers and prayer requests influence your own public prayers. And learn from church history, from the liturgy, and from prayer books how to make your prayers succinct, rich, and true.

What about the benediction? It is often a spontaneous closing prayer. A visiting preacher or elder from another church might be invited to give a closing prayer, and he summarizes the sermon, "Help us to remember . . . ." That's not bad, but the word "benediction" (Latin, *benedictus*) has to do with blessing. The "proper" way to do a benediction is with eyes open. The congregation should be looking at the one pronouncing the benediction. The benedictor would have some sort of posture whereby the people are being blessed. Looking his or her brothers and sisters in the eye, the priest (any member of the "Royal Priesthood") prays: "The Lord bless you and keep you. The Lord make His face to shine upon you. The Lord be gracious unto you. The Lord lift up His countenance upon you and give you peace. In Christ our Lord. Amen." People look up and receive the blessing.

Then comes the dismissal. The dismissal is also an important part of the service. Typically, in our churches we thoughtlessly sing a closing chorus so that the preacher can make it to the back door and shake peoples' hands. There must be a more purposeful way to end a service! You need to have a purpose for everything you do, and moving people is not a good purpose. Some worship leaders say they put as much energy if not more into the closing act because that is what is going to be running through people's minds as they leave. It's the parting shot for them. After the blessing, you need to have some way of sending them out into the world. Send them out to love and serve God. Send them empowered and ready to reenter the rough-and-tumble world. Give them hope until we meet again.

Too often what happens is, we close our eyes for a summarizing spontaneous prayer, then mindlessly sing a closing chorus while we get our things together, and we miss our great opportunity for spiritual contact.

PRAYER

How can prayer be more intentional at your church? Write down ten ideas.

1.

2.

3.

4.

5.

6.

7.

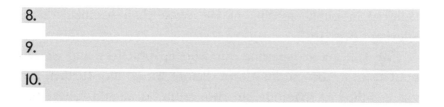

8.

9.

10.

Devotion to Scripture Reading

We have always been a people of the Book. At least, earlier generations were people of the Book. Today, we're a people who remember and pride ourselves on having been a people of the Book; we are those who used to structure our polity and policies on the Book. But, simply stated, we have stopped reading the Book! If we are to be a people of the Book, we must be devoted to the Book!

A People of the Book?

Do I overstate my case? I have brought my Bible to many Christian churches, and never had to open it. I have been in many chapel services at the Bible college where one verse was dutifully read as the core of the message (by the time I turned to it in my Bible, the reader was finished!), but the guest speaker never again referred to the verse (which ostensibly was the foundation of the message!). I have heard many sermons in which Max Lucado or Chuck Swindoll or the latest author was quoted more than the Word of God. I look around in many of these churches and notice that the people aren't bringing their Bibles to church anymore. After all, if we never use them in church, why lug that thing along? So: Are we, in fact, a people of the Book?

Let me make a case for restoring Scripture reading to a prominent place in the assembly. Perhaps you have already noticed that many liturgical churches read far more Scripture—Old Testament, New Testament, and Gospel—than many evangelical churches do. Ironically, some of those mainline churches are theologically so liberal that they don't actually believe the words in the Bible are from God; yet, they are more faithful (even if only from tradition) in public reading of His Word than so-called "Bible-believing Christians."

We talk about renewing our worship practices, and we talk about reaching people for Christ. Before we go any further, perhaps it is time to scrutinize our own faith. Do we still believe that the Word of God itself is powerful and effective, able to work in the hearts of people (Heb. 4:12)? Or is a good illustration or pop psychology or the latest spinmeister more trustworthy and powerful for modern ears? Has God's Word lost its power? Or have we lost our dependence on it?

The battle is not over KJV versus NIV, or even whether *The Message* or *The New Living Translation* is a politically correct paraphrase instead of an accurate translation. The battle is over whether we use the Word of God in the first place! To paraphrase Paul, given a choice I'd rather hear five words (whether in stilted Elizabethan English or cutesy pop compromise) from God than I would ten thousand words from mere man. Let's restore the public reading of Scripture! We are promised God's blessing if we do. In Revelation 1:3, both the reader and the hearer are pronounced blessed, indicating that the Word was meant to be publicly read. Paul told Timothy to devote himself to the public reading of Scripture (1 Tim. 4:13). We are promised that the Word of God is powerful and effective (Heb. 4:12) and that the Scriptures are able to make us perfect and complete (2 Tim. 3:16, 17). With all of these commands and promises, how can we neglect reading?

Perhaps one reason we neglect the Word in public assembly is because it is so poorly read. We watch the top of someone's head as he or she sightreads and stumbles through mispronounced words in a monotonous voice—the very words of life. But surely there must be a way to add creativity, interest, meaning, and zeal to the Word. In many liturgical churches (remember those churches that don't take God at His Word?), they use formulas just before and after the reading, such as "Give attention!" or "The Word of the Lord," with the response from the congregation, "Thanks be to God!" In many of the churches, they stand for the reading of the Gospel. Have we taken the Word more lightly by sitting inattentively with arms casu-ally folded while the very words of life are being read? How *dare* we treat the Lord's Word so contemptuously?!

THE WATER GATE REVIVAL

Let me tell you about The Great Water Gate Revival of 445 (B.C.). Or better yet, let me let God tell you about it, as found in Nehemiah chapters 8–10 (with highlights and commentary from me). This is the Word of the Lord. Give attention!

When the seventh month came and the Israelites had settled in their towns *[after returning from captivity in Babylon]*, all the people assembled as one man in the square before the Water Gate. They told Ezra the scribe to bring out the book of the Law of Moses, which the Lord had commanded for Israel. *[Though Ezra has been special-ly commissioned to teach the Law, this is the first time it is recorded that the people actu-ally asked him to read it!]*

So on the first day of the seventh month Ezra the priest brought the Law before the assembly, which was made up of men and women and all who were able to understand. *[Adults and children old enough; perhaps there was child care provided? More likely the infants stayed back with their mothers.]* He read it aloud from daybreak till noon *[four hours of Scripture reading!]* as he faced the square before the Water Gate in the presence of the men, women and others who could understand. And *all the people listened attentively to the Book of the Law. [Four hours of reading would do no good unless attentively listened to!]*

Ezra the scribe stood on a high wooden platform built for the occasion. *[Note that there was planning and preparation behind this great assembly, and they were ready for the crowds.]* Beside him on his right and on his left stood *[several people who were evidently Levites—it gives their names].*

Ezra opened the book. *[There is something of a reverent dramatic flair here.]* All the people could see him because he was standing above them; *[Did you ever wonder where the idea for an elevated platform came from? It was so that everyone could see!]* and as he opened it, the people all stood up *[This was not a time to be casual, nor to be in contrition, but a time to reverent-ly listen, and their posture indicates orderly attention].* Ezra praised the LORD, the great God; and all the people lifted their hands and respond-ed, "Amen!" *[Ezra was a worship leader, and the people experienced the word* yadah, *lifting their hands unashamedly.]* Then they bowed down and wor-shiped the Lord with their faces to the ground. *[Now comes the word* shahah *as they humble themselves.]*

The Levites . . . instructed the people in the Law while the people were standing there. They read from the Book of the Law of God, making it clear and giving the meaning so that the people could understand what was being read. *[For this lengthy reading, those other Levites took turns, and they provided running commentary, or perhaps even translation from Hebrew to Aramaic. In any case, the goal was* understanding.*]*

Then Nehemiah the governor, Ezra the priest and scribe, and the Levites who were instructing the people said to them all, "This day is sacred to the LORD your God. Do not mourn or weep." For all the people had been weeping as they listened to the words of the Law. *[When people really listen with understanding, the Law brings deep conviction. Revival was taking place from simply reading and explaining the Scriptures!]*

Nehemiah said, "Go and enjoy choice food and sweet drinks, and send some to those who have nothing prepared. This day is sacred to our Lord. Do not grieve, for the joy of the LORD is your strength."

The Levites calmed all the people, saying, "Be still, for this is a sacred day. Do not grieve." *[As is the case in every revival, first came the bad news, followed by the good news. The people were deeply convicted, humbled, and broken before the Lord, followed by great rejoicing.]*

Then all the people went away to eat and drink, to send portions of food and to celebrate with great joy, because they now understood the words that had been made known to them.

What was the source of this revival? Simply reading and explaining the Law of God to a people who were ready to listen. The results are recorded in chapter 9: After a week, the people came back and stood in their places again, again read for one fourth of the day, then confessed their sins and the sins of their ancestors, and worshiped the Lord for another fourth of the day. Then they stood up and praised the Lord—and what great rejoicing they experienced, no doubt, as they had come with desperation and found forgiveness. At the end of the lengthy prayer listed in Scripture (who says public prayers must always be brief?), they finished confessing their sins and asked the Lord for mercy with regard to their political and economic station.

But confession, worship, praise, prayer, and petition are not the end of the revival. In chapter 10, they bind themselves with a curse and an oath to follow the Lord; they put away foreign wives and idols, they pledge not to violate the Sabbath, and they promise to take care of the new temple. All in all, it was quite a time in the history of Israel, and it all started with Scripture reading.

How Can We Apply This?

Can God work that kind of powerful revival today? Do we still have the same Scriptures? The answer to both questions is "yes!" If we simply read the gospel and make it clear to the people so they can understand it, God can work revival. He brings conviction and He brings healing. He promised that His Word would never return to Him without doing its intended work (Isa. 55:10-11). So let it be!

In my worship planning, I try to include readings from the Psalms, the Old Testament, the epistles, and the Gospels. This is not rigid, and is only done to the degree that it can be done smoothly, without seeming too stilted. When we read, we try to do it creatively, with variety and preparation in the readers. The Scripture can be memorized, dramatized, or recorded. I have a friend who plays a tape on a walkman discretely hooked to his belt, and he recites a long passage to the people as he makes eye contact and speaks with dramatic flair. Choral readings, responsive readings, family readings, musical underscore, pop-up readings from the congregation, different translations, all these are ways to add creativity to the readings. And, by the way, it is a great idea to cite the page number in the pew Bibles, and to give people enough time to turn to the passage, before starting the actual reading. As they turn, you can provide some introductory remarks to set the reading in its context. Inviting people to stand, and admonishing them to "give attention" will aid intent listening as well. And please, don't invite people to fill out registration cards during Scripture reading time!

Public Scripture reading, when well done, can be the source of revival in many churches. Let us give attention!

Scripture Reading

Write down ten ideas for ways to improve the public reading of Scripture in your church's assemblies.

1.

2.

3.

4.

5.

6.

7.

8.

9.

10.

Of Preludes, Postludes, and Bumper Music

The story has happened many times: The organist (we'll call her Betty) has been practicing all week to play an appropriate piece for the Prelude. She is rightfully expecting that the saints will arrive a few minutes early, find a seat, and quietly kneel or sit and meditatively read or pray as they prepare for the assembly to begin. She has carefully chosen a piece that will enhance and guide those dear folks in their thoughts. All is ready, and Betty faithfully begins ten minutes before the appointed time.

But what's this? As she plays, she notices a sound mixing with and soon drowning out her music. It's the sound of . . . of talking.

Not just quiet whispering, intent on honoring the solitude of others; it is plain, on-the-street, out-loud, how-do-you-do silliness. And laughter, too! Betty pushes the pedal a bit to increase the volume; they take their cue and talk louder. In the meantime, those disciplined worshipers who have come to quietly meditate sit with their eyes scanning the page. On the outside they look like they are reading, but inside their heads, they are standing up and screaming, "Will somebody please SHUT UP so I can think?! If you'd pray once in a while instead of talking all the time, the Lord would teach you to be sensitive to the needs of others!"

Two, then three times they go through the cycle of turning up the volume; it's an all-out battle now. This has left all semblance of a worshipful atmosphere. Neither organist nor congregation will repent. Then Betty devises a diabolical scheme. She builds to a huge climax, forcing the congregation to fairly shout to be heard, then suddenly and unexpectedly cuts off. The silence catches Mabel yelling, "I fry mine in lard!" Betty is vindicated, and vengeance, as the Good Book says, is the Lord's.

There must be a better way to prepare for the assembly. The problem is, few congregations among evangelicals arrive prepared for respectful silence. They are simply going to visit and talk no matter what we write in our bulletin. (*The Methodist Hymnal*, 1905, writes at the beginning of their Order of Public Worship, "Let all our services begin exactly at the time appointed, and let all our people kneel in silent prayer on entering the sanctuary.") So we seem to have two options: We could plant ushers to shush the people as they enter (but that starts the service on a negative, restrictive note); or, we could just let the people talk (but that can be a potential source of irritation to those who come in quietness).

Is there another option? I'd like to propose one. Use a CD and let people visit. Here's why I propose it: 1) The idea of "preparing to worship" is theologically flawed; either you worship acceptably or you don't; you can't "prepare" to worship. 2) A CD has no feelings and takes no time to prepare. 3) Fellowship is one of the factors in public worship. We do indeed come for one another. So let's minister before the assembly, and if we are going to give directives about conversation, encourage it to be of the Lord. 4) The choice of the CD can help to subtly influence the future of worship. If you are moving in a contemporary, or more freely participative, or more reverent and classical direction, you can play music that models that style. It can even help to teach a new hymn or chorus that you plan to introduce in a few weeks. 5) It is more culturally friendly to play background music that sets a mood without sounding "churchy."

Do you have another idea, or perhaps a factor that has not already been included? If so, answer the question below.

Preludes, Postludes and Bumper Music

What do you prefer to do with the music before, after, and in spaces during the worship assembly? What are the advantages of your plan?

CHAPTER SIX

CURRENT AND FUTURE WORSHIP

THE SHIFTING PARADIGM OF WORSHIP STYLES

L et's take one more approach at getting a big picture of where worship is going in your church before we enter into how to lead it. In this chapter, we will discuss what generations are represented in your church and your community, where worship is headed in the future, and how best to reach all generations in the assembly. Lastly, we will look at the design and use of building space, and at the theological implications of architecture.

Every church has several generations in it. Each generation tends to have its own subculture, with its own view of aesthetics, of music, and of worship preferences. The better we understand the needs and the subculture of each generation, the more effective our worship will be. So at the risk of stereotyping any specific person, let's first explore the generations in your church.

If we divide a congregation into three general generations, the most common labels are **Boosters** (born before 1945), **Boomers** (born during the Baby Boom, 1945–1964) and **Busters** (born after 1964). However, we could further divide each of these larger groups into smaller subgroups (also keep in mind that different authors use different cutoff dates).

THE BOOSTERS

There are two generations of Boosters—those born before the Great Depression of 1929 (though most would tell you it was not so great!) and those born after. Those born before 1929 are sometimes labeled the **G.I. Generation**, because they were of age during World War II. Now they are moving into "elder emeritus" status in our churches (whether with a title or not, they are mostly out of positions of influence now). Those born 1930–1945 could be called the **Builders**, because they set up the current culture. They might remember the depression years and the war years, but they were too young to have experienced it as adults. Many of this generation are just now moving into retirement age, and are considered "older elders" in churches (as a whole, most are probably beyond the peak of their influence in most churches).

Elmer Towns describes the tendencies of this generation.[1] He says that if Boosters would have a slogan, it might be *Make the best of what you have.* They respect and wish to preserve tradition, to save their money, and to avoid risk. They tend to be patriotic and loyal to an organization (whether family, church, or job). They tend to be conservative in doctrine and in emotional expression. Their worship preferences are more formal and meditative, with organ-and-hymn-centered music, and they do not respond well to constant change. They would rather watch and listen than stand, clap, and discuss. Their heart music (most likely the music they heard the most between the ages of 10 and 13)[2] is sentimental ballads (with chromatic harmonies and added sixths) and uplifting march tunes (with a lilt and an emphasis on beats one and three). If they grew up in the church, they like hymns and gospel songs modeled after the nineteenth-century gospel songs.

MEETING THE WORSHIP NEEDS OF THE BOOSTERS

Let me make an appeal for meeting the needs of these senior saints. For some reason, our society idolizes youth and despises old age. Instead of honoring and listening to the older members of our churches,³ we have ignored and judged them. Many of the younger generations even judge them as being unspiritual, as standing in the way of "God's" progressive programs, and as being, well, an embarrassment to us.

But please try to get in their shoes for just a moment. They grew up in a different world. Everywhere they turn, things change— and obviously, no one is asking them if they like it or not. The local grocery store is now enlarged and reorganized into a huge mega-lopolis, where you have to hike two miles past lawn mowers, photo finishing, and sushi bars just to get milk and eggs (remember them?). Maybe you can find one radio station with the music they grew up with, if you live in a big enough city. TV is filled with graphic scenes of sex and violence, and rock music, with images bombarding the senses and geared for younger, polyphasic minds. Even baseball, the great American leisurely summer pastime, has transmogrified into some multisensory, rock-'n'-roll, onslaught of commercials and sensuality.

Is there no place where life and faith and the pace of life is the same? Surely the church, built on the Rock of Ages who never changes, preaching the Old Jerusalem gospel, would be the lasting refuge of tradition and normalcy. But no, now they've hired some young idealistic song leader who makes us stand for half an hour, clap our hands, see the screen, and listen to the blare of in-escapable driving music. Hymns are out, the organ is gone, and nothing looks or sounds the same. Then they pressure us to give for the renovation project, in which they will install a screen, new lighting, and sound equipment, and take away the communion table and the organ.

Considering all that these seniors are asked to endure, is it any wonder that some in the older generations resist what some call "progress" and "cultural relevance" (to whose culture?)?

Maybe if they really opened up to tell you why they seem to be unspiritual and to resist your plans, they would say this:

> My knees do not let me stand up and sit down so easily, and the move-able chairs provide no anchor to help me up. I just can't get the rhythm of

those choruses, and there is no notated music for me to learn the tune the way I'm used to. And when I don't feel the beat, I can't begin to clap the way the younger people do. Frankly, my bladder will allow me to be in the room for only an hour, and I become very uncomfortable with the unpredictability of the service. My bifocals don't help me to read the screen, and there's nothing in my hands to read. And my eardrums, supplemented with a hearing aid, do not respond with the resilience of your youthful ears to the loudness of the music. I'm not unspiritual, I really am not. I want to reach new people for Christ, and I'm willing to pay a price to do it. But you have forced all of these changes on me, and never once asked me. And now you judge me for speaking up on the silent roll call card, or for resisting changes by voting against them in a congregational vote, or for sitting near the back, as far from the speakers as I can. I just want to remind you that I've still come faithfully, given faithfully, smiled and prayed for you, and held back my criticism. All I'm asking for is some understanding.

If we are going to reach everyone for Christ, let's be the hands and feet of Christ to every member of His Body. Let's heed the commandments to honor our fathers and mothers and respect the elderly in our midst.

THE BOOMERS

The second major generation in your church is the Baby Boomers. Again, I think that Boomers can be divided into **Early Boomers** (the Elvis / Sputnik / Howdy-Doody generation, born 1945–1955) and the **Late Boomers** (the Beatles / Apollo / Beaver generation, born 1955–1964). As Boomers were growing up, they experienced civil unrest, and were the lower half of a major "generation gap."[4] Many rejected tradition and created a counterculture in the quest to build their own utopian society.

The slogan for the Boomers is *If it's worth doing, it's worth doing right.* They have the money, and they want quality, whether in coffee or in worship music. Compared to previous generations, Boomers tend to be less committed to a job, more independent thinkers, and are more likely not to believe in absolute truth. They are more transient, relocating for employment, more likely to divorce, and more isolated from their neighbors. Women are far more career-oriented, and currently they fill their schedules with various leisure activities and sports commitments for themselves and their children. Boomers are less dogmatic and more tolerant of other belief systems. That means there is less denominational or congregational loyalty.

In their worship preferences, Boomers will tend to dress more casually, be less committed to Sunday night church or Wednesday evening activities, and prefer informal atmospheres. They prefer choruses over hymns (what we might now call "classic" choruses), and choose guitar and keyboards in a worship band.

Meeting the Worship Needs of the Boomers

Society has catered to the Boomers, for monetary and commercial reasons if nothing else. So Boomers have won the culture war, and currently they control TV, movies, and radio.[5] So if the church does not speak their cultural language, they are unlikely to stay in great numbers. They will go to the megachurch across town that is attracting Boomers like a porch light draws moths on a summer night.

A Boomer church will have no choir, no organ, and probably no piano. It will be guitar-driven and band-centered, and will be high-touch and high-tech. Small groups in homes have replaced Sunday night and Wednesday night services and Bible School hour. Expository sermons (which start from Scripture) have been replaced with felt-needs-based topical series. Boomers do not want more guilt—they already feel plenty of it. They want practical answers and hope. They look for a church that emanates an aura of success, which is usually measured in numbers (growing attendance, finances, and programs). They want to know how to raise their children, and are looking for programs that will meet the social and spiritual needs of the family members. Their music style is mostly soft rock and country.

THE BUSTERS (GENX)

The Baby Busters can likewise be divided into three groups. America had a Baby Bust from 1965–1976, especially 1973–1975 (perhaps due to early Boomers delaying starting a family, to planning for smaller families, to abortion, or to the general angst of the age?). Those adults are sometimes now called **Busters**. But after that, there was an Echo Boom, and births have been up for several years. Those born 1972–1981 have most often been called Generation X, or **GenX**, sometimes also called the millennial generation, as they are coming into adulthood at the turn of the millennium. Then those born since 1981 are sometimes designated as **Generation Y**. Distinctions can be made between these three groups, as Busters are the MTV/PC/Reagan-Bush generation, and GenX is the Internet/Postmodern/Clinton generation. Of course, those born since 1982 have their own identity, and it is just now emerging. But it will be some time until they can definitively be categorized.

What marks the people of Post-Boomer years? Well, they were raised by Boomers, so many were largely unsupervised as children; the latchkey kids of divorced parents, growing up in day care and not receiving consistent discipline. Or, on the other end of the spectrum, they were raised by stay-at-home, back-to-nature, home-schooling parents who were very involved in their lives. Busters have been a great experiment in political correctness, part of which is self-esteem without discipline (starting with Sesame Street and going through school with no corporal punishment), and part of which is the doctrine of toleration. While Boomers tend toward group think as a generation, Busters tend to group themselves into "villages" of sub- and countercultural cliques. Busters know more than any previous generation about new technology, but they are less skilled in basic academics. They are more entertainment and leisure oriented, and they have much more interest in "real" relationships than in organizations and programs. Their religion must be based on relationships, practical application, and tolerance. They have grown up with a certain cynicism and pessimistic despair. The Internet is their window to the world, and they have access to an incredible amount of information. Their music stands in stark contrast to that of their grandparents, especially in the area of "beauty" of voice. They resist "cheesy" romance and easy answers. They are service oriented to a cause they can believe in; they think globally and act locally. But at the same time, they do not easily take up any cause, just on the argument that it "ought" to be done or that it has "always" been done. GenX-ers especially have the ability, whether from being young or being of that culture, to leap from the absurd to the profound instantly. They seldom consider whether something seems proper to the occasion, whether clothing or humor. GenX is especially sensitive to be inclusive (beyond just being tolerant) with other cultures. Identity, community, and meaning are three key words to the GenX culture. Lastly, and ironically, they are individuals, not a group, and so "they" don't like to be stereotyped (which we have just done here).

How do these marks affect the worship preferences of the post-Boomer? They don't prefer "traditional" worship, and they don't prefer "contemporary" worship (if "contemporary" means "Boomer style"). Really the choice is not twofold (traditional versus contemporary), but is at least threefold (Booster *versus* Boomer *versus* Buster). Buster songs are not structured traditionally—each song has its own set of rules and its own aesthetic for sound and lyrics. World music, which eclectically reflects and combines many cultures, is seen as preferable. Surprisingly, many GenXers are also rediscovering mystical aspects of ancient worship practices, and many are turning to historical and mysterious aspects of programming.

Meeting the Worship Needs of the Busters

How to describe GenX worship? My friend Ted Troxell (a Buster) describes the difference between Boomer and GenX worship this way:

[Boomer worship is] programmed. One of [the goals of Boomer worship]—spoken or unspoken—was that the service would flow pretty much like a newscast. No seams. Start on time, end on time. There's a certain "slickness," a polished excellence. Boomer worship is performance-oriented, based on the culture of corporate America. Bill Hybels said that when people drive onto the WC campus, they should feel like they could just as well be at the IBM headquarters in Atlanta. The music style is adult contemporary. They love media, and are usually impressed by technology. Preaching? Motivational, how-to stuff. They love lists: "four ways to overcome fear," etc. Expectation of their leaders? They are powerful, effective role models. Not necessarily perfect, but it would be nice. Again, they want "excellence," and that means it looks nice and tidy and neat.

Enter the Buster. To him, that's all fake. Smoke and mirrors. Stupid plastic smiles on the [worship] team. He's leery of institutions to begin with. Programming takes a backseat to organic structures. He doesn't want slickness, he wants sincerity. He doesn't want a performance (which doesn't mean he doesn't want to be entertained), he wants a relationship (even though Busters lack relationship skills). AC music? Ho-hum. He'll respond better to some sort of "unplugged" kind of sound, or more of a garage band. Forget corporate America. It sucks. The IBM headquarters is just a reminder that the Boomers got all the cool jobs that the next generation will get when they die. Media, shmedia. Technology is cool but he's not impressed by it. It's something he uses. Preaching? Narrative, storytelling. He loves Garrison Keillor. "Four ways to overcome fear?" Okay, he says, but tell me which two actually worked for you. Expectation of their leaders? Honesty, usually the brutal kind. He wants to be sure that you'll bleed if he sticks you with a pin. And he just might. X'ers want "real," and to them that reality is dark, seamy, and cynical. "Gritty" is a word I like to use. I speak for my generation when I say, "I wouldn't be so cynical if reality didn't keep proving me right."

Here's an irony of change in Boomers: back in the early '60s, many of them were "into" folk music (coffee houses, Bob Dylan, Smothers Brothers, Peter, Paul, and Mary), which was guitar-based and featured intimate settings. As the '60s progressed, and especially into the '70s and beyond, the taste of culture changed, and Boomers became enamored with technology and slick shows. Lights, multimedia, choreography, and major musical forces (BS&T, Moody Blues, and the BeeGee's) influenced their aesthetic. Once Boomers began to set the agenda in the church in the '80s, they embraced these big production approaches in their worship. The irony is that today GenX is going right back to coffee houses and guitar-based, folk music (usually considered alternative). What's old is new again. Just when the Boomers finally take over the direction of the church, the party has moved on from major productions and slick presentations to more intimate settings, and more spontaneous, less performance-based ministry. So, while Boomers flock to the megachurch with its slick programming, Busters are going to relational cell-based churches.

Truly, Post-Contemporary Worship is "ancient-future" worship. Candlelight and simple acoustic settings are enhanced with alternative rock music and high-tech projectors. All worship practices of all times in history are now open to borrow from freely, as fits the moment. And so Byzantine icons (downloaded from the internet) are used, but not as the orthodox would use them. And Celtic music is the rage, but not as the Irish would do it. The only rule is that it must feel "authentic." What is authentic? No one knows, but GenX-ers will tell you that they can tell a fake immediately. Fake is prepackaged arrangements (we will sing this through three times with a tag), easy answers, shallow lyrics, cheesy music, and autopilot leaders. Silence, community, flexibility, vulnerable transparency, and new discoveries are authentic.

Reflection/Application

1. If you were the worship leader for a church of Boosters, describe in three sentences what you might do in your worship style to best minister to them.
2. If you were the worship leader for a church that purposely targeted Boomers, describe in three sentences what you might do in your worship style to best minister to them.
3. If you were planning worship for a church of Busters, describe in three sentences what you might do in your worship style to best minister to them.
4. If you were facilitating worship for a GenX church, describe in three sentences what you might do in your worship style to best minister to them.

Worldview Paradigm Shifts

Each church has six or seven generations in its membership. Each church probably also has different worldviews represented by its members. Historically, we have thought that there was a two-way division between liberal modernists and conservative heartlanders.[6] The modernists are materialists, humanists, and functional atheists, although they may belong to a mainline denomination. They are most likely Democrats. They are the enemies of the conventional, right-wing conservative, family-values-espousing Republican Christians. But an even bigger paradigm shift today is the worldview often called postmodernism. It is not family-value conservative. It is also not modernist liberal. The postmodern mind-set is going in a new direction, liberal in most ways, but rooted in Nature and "Green values," in religious mysteries and spiritual matters, in community and shifting truth.

The church must learn to change and speak the language of postmodern, post-Enlightenment, post-Christian society, if we are going to make an impact on the world. We must be aware of the needs of every generation and its subcultures if we are going to meet needs. And we must anticipate where the next paradigm shift is going, that we might tell the next generation about the goodness of the Lord.

Worship NeXt

What will future worship look like? We all want to know that, mostly so that we can be on the cutting edge (Becky Ahlberg calls it the "bleeding edge") of trends. Will worship be more multisensory? More symbolic? More blended? What does postcontemporary music sound like? More GenX traits? Or will the pendulum swing back, as it did for the Boomers, toward performance and polish? Or, perhaps, will an outside force interrupt the natural transition of the development of worship styles, such as economic or political crisis causing the church to go underground? I am going to be so bold as to make a few predictions about the worship of the NeXt generation.

FUTURE TRENDS

Andrew Greeley had predicted the current trends in worship more than 30 years ago.[7] Trends lean toward *acceptance, authenticity, individualistism, music–driven, mystically sexual,* and *multisensory*. These trends may well continue into the foreseeable future.

The next worship trend will be toward full *acceptance* of other expressions and styles. The current interest in "world music" is likely to continue—not that Americans want to immerse themselves in another culture, but they do want to "sample" and affirm all cultures of the world. The current climate of tolerance, nonjudgmental acceptance, political correctness, and individual expression runs deep in the values of younger generations. Of course, there are dangers. Nonbelievers are invited to find common ground worshiping with the saints, and no distinction is apparent between them. Sin is deemphasized and mercy and love are the focus. The worship song of the future will be, "I'm okay, you're okay, the Lover loves us anyway."

Worship of the present and future must have *authenticity*. By that, it somehow must come across as natural, not contrived, relevant, "real," and even somewhat unpolished. Current trends in music are toward asymmetry, unrhymed lyrics, and an almost improvisatory character. The opinion of John Cotton in the preface to the 1640 *Bay Psalm Book* seems to capture the current mindset: *Gods Altar needs not our pollishings*. No doubt, there will be a backlash from this trend, and there will be a highly-refined professional "worship recording industry," as is already in place. In the future, look for more semichanting of Scripture, and of spontaneous songs improvised over static harmonies.

Worship will probably continue along the lines of being very *individualistic*. With great freedom and acceptance, worshipers will choose when and how to participate, with the musicians increasingly off to the side or in the back of the worship space. The worship leader will be more perceived as a "lead worshiper," without manipulative directives. Ultimately, the danger is that the worshiper becomes the measure of truth, and even becomes the center of the focus of worship. The worship song of the future will be, "I'm coming back to the heart of worship, and it's all about me."

Possibly, worship will continue to be *music-driven*, as it now is. Note how often the singing time is called the worship time, and how often a musician is called the worship minister. Chuck Fromm has called music the new sacrament of the postmodern church. At the same time, in the future there is likely to be a pendulum swing back to nonmusical expressions of worship, as we rediscover historical and biblical balance. I do suspect that the current guitar-driven style, with its simple and subtle harmonies will swing back to keyboard-influenced music, and that music will again be more harmonically complex. Of course, more ethnic instruments will be added to the church arsenal, as well.

This one may be controversial, but a current trend is more and more for worship to be *mystically sexual*.[8] Of course, worshipers are not going to participate in overt sexual activity in public worship, but many of today's songs use sexual language in their expressions of devotion and worship.[9] The Pietists of four centuries ago sang often of their relationship as Bride to the Bridegroom. In the same way today, it seems that a significant number of songs recently have been love songs. The danger, as already mentioned, is that often the deity is unspecified, and only the context makes it a Christian worship song. In the future, there will be an increase in "worship crossover" songs, played on secular radio as love songs and sung in the church as worship songs. The songs will crossover both ways, as seeker-oriented churches use secular songs,[10] and as popular "worship concert bands" are marketed in secular venues.

Worship of the future will likewise be *multisensory*. Technology will combine with the ancient in a display of scent, lighting, art, mystery, and symbol. Teaching will increasingly be multimedia, with video and visual imagery enhancing the presentations, and worship leaders will need to have acumen in staging, lights, and interior design. In the near future, rock music will combine with meditative drones and candles, incense and visual displays, and worshipers will participate with much exuberant gesture and dance and posturing.

In the future, worship will serve as the primary apologetic for the gospel, as society moves farther from rational arguments and into Postmodernism. Worship serves as the mysterious experience of immersion into how a truth "feels," rather than reasoning how a truth "makes sense." The experience of worship will bring the sense of the very Presence of God, and that requires no words or explanations. Postmodernism and New Age merge in *contemplative*, though not necessarily quiet, mystical insight. Truth is perceived, not on the rational, cognitive level, but deeply perceived, nonetheless.[11]

Two Divergent Paths?

I believe that worship within the next generation in America will go one of two directions, or more probably both at the same time: on the one hand, churches will explore mystery, symbolism, and the arts, and will borrow eclectically from various worship traditions.[12] At the same time, churches will continue to offer common-ground spiritual experiences to reach seekers.[13] Those churches that already have buildings and facilities will continue to grow, and they will be marked by polished presentation in large group happenings. But more and more church plants will not be able to afford, or will not be able to obtain zoning for, a facility of their own, and I believe that we will see a rise in small group, house church, relational, internet-enhanced, prayer-oriented, charismatic, historical worship.

Let me go into a little more detail. There is increasing fascination with other cultures and traditions, and as today's children become tomorrow's leaders, their politically correct upbringing will equip them to create an experience that is more eclectic and more tolerant of the practices of other people of faith. Some churches, seeking to be evangelical, will continue the trend toward common-ground worship experience, and they will lessen the distinction between Christian worship and a generic spiritual (or emotional) experience. These churches will use the arts and symbolism to proclaim the gospel in nonoffensive terms, and worship will function much as did Jesus' parables. For those who have ears to hear, truth about Christ will be clearly presented, but until such time as people can understand it, the assembly functions more as religious mystery. These groups will invent a non-Roman version of the catholic church, minus the vestments, the tradition, and the doctrinal distinctives. Eventually, when the political situation changes, these will be registered churches, officially able to continue as tax exempt institutions and offering faith-based humanitarian services to their communities.

Other churches will take a more isolationist approach. They will also, no doubt, borrow indiscriminately from other worship traditions, but their worship will be more countercultural, small-group based, and more conservative. These churches will be persecuted, at least financially (no zoning variants, taxed status, etc.). They will be largely family-based and neighborhood-centered, and they will use Internet and other communications systems to keep a sense of community with one another. The worship will be more prayer-driven, and the church will be smaller and more radical. *Charismata* and expressiveness will definitely rise in these churches.

In both types of churches, the current trend away from ministerial training at seminary or Bible college will continue. Much future church leadership will come from anointed leaders rather than seminary-trained leaders. Model churches will serve as training ground for others, and many church leaders will be raised up through apprenticeships in local churches. Communication will continue to expand, and alternative equipping centers will rise. Today's liberal churches, based on rationalistic modernism, will virtually cease to exist in two generations. But today's conservatives will become more theologically liberal in the next generation, as postmodern Christians make up their own hermeneutic from the smorgasbord of choices available to them.[14]

Worship leaders of the last generation were church musicians, who had choral music training and a smattering of professional churchmanship. Worship leaders of the current generation are natural "pop" musicians, with skills in shaping the emotional and spiritual experience of a crowd. Worship leaders of tomorrow's seeker churches will be creative artists with excellent crowd skills. Worship leaders of tomorrow's radical underground churches will be men and women of spiritual influence, whether with strong musical skills or not.

Reflection/Application

Give your response/opinion. Of the elements of psychedelia that Andrew Greeley says would mark worship in the year 2000, about which of them do you agree with him? Mark as many as apply. (Of course, there are no wrong answers here; it's opinion only).

❑ Ecstatic
❑ Using rock music
❑ Engaging all the senses
❑ Nonrational
❑ Some combination of rhythm and blues and gospel music ("a combination of sensualism and near-hysterical enthusiasm")
❑ Contemplative, though not necessarily quiet
❑ Aims at mystical insight
❑ Symbolic, ceremonial and ritualistic
❑ Communitarian ("relationship-oriented, with small groups and an emphasis on 'natural,' 'out front,' 'honest,' 'authentic,' and 'spontaneous.'")
❑ Profoundly sexual

Explain one (or more) of your responses above. In what way do you agree or disagree with Greeley on current trends in cultural worship in America today?

Specialized Services or Blended Worship?

Many churches lately have been opting for targeted worship services. The concept of "targeted" services is to design the music and program for a narrower "market audience" than the multi-generational church has done. Are targeted services working? Are they wise? Let's explore them.

How did most churches come to the place of targeted services in the first place? Some are church plants, but many are established congregations, which have been moving slowly from traditional to blended worship style. They see that contemporary churches near them are growing much faster than they are. Within the congregation, there is resistance from the older members who pressure them not to change any faster, and there is pressure from the younger members to update worship styles more quickly. Having two (or more) specialized services seems to be the practical approach to make each camp happy.

Choose Your Style

If you are going to create targeted services, be sure to study the demographics and style of your targeted group(s). Of course, "traditional" and "contemporary" are relative terms, depending on the subculture of the particular church and its community. Usually, it is most effective to make the early service traditional (older, committed folks will come to the early time slot), and make the later service contemporary (younger folks like to sleep in; besides, loud, driving music and early mornings don't seem to mix as well, according to Proverbs 27:14!).[15]

More recently, many churches are also opting for GenX targeted services. GenX services are often offered on Saturday or Sunday evenings, in a coffeehouse-type of setting, with "unplugged" music up front. The worship participation is optional for those in attendance, recognizing that interpersonal connectedness is a higher priority than having everyone sing or do motions or listen to what is coming from up front.

Some churches go so far as to offer targeted services featuring country western music, or intergenerational family-friendly services, and so forth. Unity is maintained by having all of the specialized services under the oversight of one eldership.

Pros and Cons

Targeted services answer several problems for churches. In a word, they grow. Numbers increase as people come to the assembly with a worship style that speaks their heart language. Targeted services seem to make the gospel more relevant to the cultural milieu of a subgroup within the community. They also resolve some of the tension over trying to blend musical styles to keep everyone happy.

Many churches that have gone the route of targeted services have found, however, that there is also a down side to targeted services. I have spoken with music ministers who have been part of targeted services, and of the fairly small sample that I have had exposure to, they describe a pattern that is frighteningly uniform.

Central Church's Story: Beginnings

Here is a composite of the typical pattern that I hear: Central Church runs about 300 in attendance. Growth has been slow, and there is resistance from some folks to the idea of becoming more "contemporary." So, they decide to add a second service. The early service becomes more traditional, and the later one is contemporary. The sermon is the same for both services, but the worship style is very different. The second service will use drama, a rock band, and projected words; the first service has organ, piano, and choir.

People are given the vision for the services ahead of time, and within a few weeks of the kickoff, the balance begins to emerge. The church runs about 200 in the traditional service, and 100 in the contemporary service. The instrumentalists for the early service are already in place, but some recruiting and training yet needs to be done for the contemporary assembly. Also, the second service needs to find its "personality" yet; the staging, lights, mikes, sound mix, rehearsal, and personnel need to be trained, and the vocabulary and personality of the entire service needs to become more consistent and seeker-friendly. It's not business as usual anymore! Contemporary worship often requires more staging, more use of media, and more drama and energy, and far more communication and planning. But there is hope of new life, and everybody is feeling pretty good about the new service.

Six months into the split services, the church is even more excited, and the elders feel that they have made the wisest decision in the life of the church. The contemporary service has grown to 150, and the first service is still pretty well holding its own; attendance there has slipped down to 180, with a few of the folks finding that they prefer the creativity of the contemporary hour. For the sake of their family, some extended families all attend the later service. Overall, Central Church is now running 330—a ten percent growth rate in only six months.

After a year, all seems to be even healthier. The contemporary service now has a full band in place, and the momentum is starting to build there as the leadership gels. The second service is now at 185, and the first service is 175. (Do you see something developing here?) Twenty percent growth in one year!

Challenges Arise

After two years, some discontent begins to arise. The contemporary service has reached the 250 mark, while the first service is now down to 150. Central Church itself has experienced rapid growth, having grown 33% in just two years, but the price is that it seems to be becoming two groups. As reality begins to set in, the honeymoon comes to an end.

Here are some problems that are beginning to surface:

5 **Music minister burnout.** After two years of a doubled work load, the responsibility is beginning to wear on the music minister.

ϟ **Divided loyalty.** The people in the traditional service begin to sense divided devotion from the staff. Jesus said, "No one can serve two masters. He will love the one and hate the other, or else be devoted to the one and despise the other." The traditionalists don't feel loved anymore.

ϟ **Inequity.** Money and energy are channeled into the second service, while creativity wanes in the first service. The first service now is the hour for "playing it safe" in order to avoid problems, and the second hour is the time to take risks and be creative.

ϟ **Criticism.** Whenever numbers go up, enthusiasm goes up; but when numbers in a church are depressed, people tend to become critical. So, the traditional service people start to talk about the little irritations they have had for the last two years: *Why do we have to look at those drums up front, when we never use them and don't want them?* And, *Why do they need that ugly stack of amplifiers, that screen and theatrical lighting, drama sets and other changes to the auditorium, when they have no place in our assembly?*

ϟ **Shift in Power.** Most of the money comes from the traditional group, but the contemporary group can outvote them. Most of the elders attend the traditional service, but the contemporary group uses up the most staff time, counseling time, benevolence needs, etc. Tension sets in as the inequity outweighs the original vision.

What seemed to be a great idea for the cause of evangelism now has become an irritant. Jesus said that the greatest mark of the disciples would be their love for one another, but that love has become strained.

Now let's trace the growing problem to the five-year mark. There are now two contemporary services (one contemporary and one blended or perhaps the other is GenX), running 200 each, while the traditional service is down to only about 80, a shortened chapel service that meets at 8:00 in the morning.

TRYING TO RESTORE UNITY

Finally, the decision is made that something needs to be done to restore unity at Central Church. The elders try to put the toothpaste back into the tube: they call for the church to have multiple blended worship services. When they do, they inadvertently plant New Hope Church, as many of the contemporary folk leave. Or, the contemporary megachurch up the road grows by another 200. It takes years to try to heal and restore an evangelistic vision in the remaining group at Central Church.

You see, some people feel more loyalty to a style of music than they do to their shepherds. So when criticism or correction comes from those spiritual overseers, many will go elsewhere rather than submit. The church finds itself in the very awkward position of trying to keep peace in a divided house.

Churches used to split over issues of church polity, doctrine, budgets, and leadership. But the "new sectarianism is a sectarianism of worship style. The new sectarian creeds are dogmas of music. Worship seminars are the seminaries of the new sectarianism; their directors are its theologians. The ministers of the new sectarianism are our church worship leaders."[16] If Paul were writing to the Corinthian church today, he might say, "In the first place, I hear that when you come together as a church, there are divisions among you, and to some extent I believe it" (1 Corinthians 11:18). He might further write, "You are still worldly. For since there is jealousy and quarreling among you, are you not worldly? Are you not acting like mere men? For when one says, 'I follow [the organ],' and another, "I follow [the band],' are you not mere men?" (1 Corinthians 3:3,4, my insertions).

THREE THINGS TO THINK ABOUT

Are you considering targeted worship? If so, be sure to think about these things:

1. **Think about the Music Director.** A music director's workload more than doubles with targeted services. It is not just adding another service; it is adding a whole new way of work-

ing with music. The musical leader must be versant in the musical language of traditional musicians who read from notes in one service, and of pop players who read from charts or play by ear in the other service. Wearing two hats wears on the heart and the body, and the music minister heads for burnout. Few music ministers are equally qualified in both languages, with equal vision for two worship sets each weekend.

2. **Think about Extended Families.** Many people come to church in families, and targeted worship services force grandparents, parents, and children to make impossible choices if they want to stay together. Rather than the family coming together and experiencing the unity of compromise and considering one another, we force one generation to win and the other to lose. Or else the family comes at different hours and perhaps reports back to one another later.[7]

3. **Think about the Future.** The preacher who starts the targeted worship will most likely not be the one to finish it. Whether in two years or thirty years, he will be gone, and the two subchurches will now have to agree on a new leader. That means that the new person coming in has to be accepted by what is, in effect, two very different congregations. If tenuous unity was maintained through one man's ministry, the hiring of a new leader often exacerbates the tension.

How to Avoid the Problems

These problems of targeted worship are serious. So, what can be done to avoid or lessen the problems of having two or more cultures meeting in one building? Let me make four suggestions.

1. **Stay traditional and slowly die.** This is not a good option. Perhaps one of the others will be better!

2. **Plant a new church, starting in the same building.** Rather than having an "accidental" church plant in five years, set a projected timetable for when the new congregation will become independent. If "traditional" worship is destined to die with the current older generation, then the original congrega-

tion may be signing its own death warrant by starting a new contemporary one (depending on the community), but a vibrant new church will be a planned addition.

3. **Blend the worship and change slowly.** Purposefully move toward contemporary, but keep the church together. The church may not grow as quickly (perhaps running 320 after a year instead of 360), but families stay together, and Christian unity and love is modeled before the world. I recommend this to any church leadership that is considering dividing in order to multiply: Prayerfully read Acts and the letters of Paul again, asking yourselves whether catering to specialization within the Body of Christ is the New Testament model. Remember, Jesus said that *any* house divided against itself will not stand. See the next section for some specific advice on moving forward with a blended style.

4. **Start a new church.** Let that new church be in a "targeted" area not covered by the present church. For example, many predominantly white churches would be wise to plant new works in predominantly Hispanic or Black neighborhoods, or urban works could spin off a satellite in the growing suburbs. Let each church have its own personality, speaking the language of the new people you want to reach.

Of course, this matter of changing culture in our communities needs to be addressed. The church must change over years to meet the people who live near it. It would be foolish for church leadership to bury their collective head in the sand and pretend that the challenge doesn't exist. But how to stay united and still be culturally relevant is a challenge that requires the guidance of the Holy Spirit to meet. May you have wisdom as you consider your options.

Blending Your Worship Successfully

A blended worship style may be wise, even if you have a specific target congregation. In the past, many evangelical denominations were torn apart by the disagreement over mechanical musical instruments in the assembly, or over theological liberalism. In today's culture, those matters seem to be less critical in most churches than music style. We disagree on whether to use the style of the culture outside of the church building or to minister to those who are already in the church. We are divided over ideology, over generational differences, and over musical taste. Perhaps a purposeful blending of musical styles can help bring us together.

A further challenge is that many music ministers are better versed in one "musical language" over another, so you may be lacking in strong leadership in a particular style. If your worship leader reads from chord charts but can't read printed notation, hymns and orchestras and choirs will always be a musical challenge. On the other hand, a musician who has been traditionally trained to read printed notation may be intimidated by chord charts and improvisation.

How do you "blend" a service? Start with a clear notion of where your congregation truly is. Sometimes we think that people's tastes are different than they really are because there are a few outspoken voices of perhaps prominent members.[18] Anecdotally, you can get an idea by objectively listening and watching during congregational singing to see what they relate to the most.[19] For a more objective measurement, you may want to distribute a survey to your congregation, seeking their favorite songs that were sung over the last six months (it's best to give them a specific list of recent, familiar songs). Ask for a few significant demographics (such as age grouping) to help you interpret your findings, but protect their anonymity.

Next, use your material from the first two chapters to determine the direction your church's leadership purposefully wants to move in your music. The change may only be slight, or it may be radical. Furthermore, determine together your time frame for change; do you want to move that direction over a six-month period, or perhaps a five-year period?

One way to accomplish blending is to have multiple worship teams, each of which has a different style. One group may be more gospel music, one may lean toward hymns, one may be keyboard-driven contemporary, and one may be guitar-driven. Overall, the congregation experiences a variety of styles, but in any given week the musical style may be more focused. To use terminology from an earlier chapter, different teams may each have a different "color" to their worship leading.

Another way to blend your music style is to have different styles represented among the members of your worship planning team. Be purposeful in inviting folks with different musical tastes onto your planning team.

Or, plan in sets, each of which features a different style. The opening set may be celebratory praise songs, the second set may contain high church hymns and the third set could be guitar-driven soft choruses. Touch on everyone's heart language sometime in the service. Everyone eats, but no one gets a whole loaf, as my friend Mike Shannon says.

Blended approach to worship must be openly and verbally supported from the pulpit and should be mentioned regularly. Everyone must understand the overriding philosophy for worship planning. We embrace our differences, and we value each person here. We therefore give to each person a gift of blessing in song. Thus, in our song, we demonstrate a picture of the Body of Christ in action.

Reflection/Application

In theory (not necessarily in practice), do you think it is reasonable to try to have targeted assemblies, under the umbrella of unity of a central eldership? Can you think of any scriptural support for the concept?

Now in actual practice (where real people live), do you think it is possible? If so, can you cite any scriptural principles that apply? If not, try to cite scriptural principles as well.

Have you ever seen the kinds of problems with targeted services that are described in this chapter? (Just indicate
yes or no. Of course, there are no wrong answers here.)

❑ Yes
❑ No

What do you think is the strongest "pro" for special-
ized/targeted services?

What do you see as the worst "con" about targeting
services instead of having everyone meet together?

Of Money and Buildings: The Theology of Architecture

What does your worship center design say about your philosophy of worship? There is a theological implication to every
building—to every room. We may not have thought through the
theology, but I want to think with you about the implications of
your building.

Some buildings imply by their design that they were built for
Somebody bigger than you and me. Some of these are beautiful
cathedrals, but the beauty is not to impress people with human
accomplishment; it is to point to God. Stained glass windows three
floors up diffuse light and tell holy stories. So the worshipers gaze at
the windows and steeple (which used to be the most prominent element of a town's skyline) and are pointed to God. Congregations that
have been in existence for many generations may have slowly saved
for and built such edifices as landmarks and centers of a town.

But many evangelical churches have been built in only one generation, perhaps as monuments to one man's ministry, so their buildings are much less expensive. The theology and balance of teaching is more concerned, generally, with growing in numbers and with pouring money into programs rather than aesthetics. The building is designed for the purpose of study, or perhaps of recreation (in the case of a family life center), not of worship, prayer, or artistic expression.[20] It is functional art at its most obvious, seeking as much room for people per dollar as possible.

Architecture implies theology. Your building implies your doctrine. What are the focal centers of attention in your building? Is your eye drawn to the baptistry? To the pulpit? To the table? To the stage? To the screen? To musicians? These focal points of attention imply your church's theological emphases.

There tend to be three balanced focal centers in Christian churches and churches of Christ: pulpit, baptistry, and Table. For many, they are in line vertically with each other, with the baptistry in the back of and above the pulpit and the communion table in front of it.

Some churches are built in the shape of a cross (cruciform shape). Others are in a circle, implying unity of people. Others are designed like an auditorium or concert hall. Seeker churches are built to look like a theater, with no hint of religion whatsoever. They probably have no pulpit on the stage, no cross, no baptistry, and no banners visible. There is only an auditorium with theater seating, sloped floor, stage lights, curtain, and so forth. The neutral or "secular" environment avoids offending unchurched people with churchly symbols.

In the early 1800s, from New York to Tennessee, revival was sweeping across the American frontier. So was the evangelism of Charles G. Finney. He recommended an innovation to church buildings so as to improve evangelism, and it came to be the standard for evangelical churches for almost two centuries. Instead of the congregation sitting in a box shape to face one another, with the pulpit on one side of the building, the stage area was moved to one end, and all of the seats turned to face the same way. The choir was located behind the pulpit, so that the musicians served as coproclaimers with the preacher. An evangelistic invitation was offered at the end of the sermon, and the penitent came to the front while a song was sung. For the first time in the history of the Church, Sunday morning became a time for evangelism, rather than for worship. The theological shift made the earlier building design impractical, and form soon followed function.

Does the form of your building follow the function of your mission? Is your building consistent with the choices you made back in chapter two? Does your building draw attention to God, draw the believers together, or draw the lost in the same proportions as your mission statement? When your building agrees with your mission, it is an asset to your purpose.

If you are in a building program, let your theology dictate your architecture, rather than an architect who might not understand your values.[21] Don't just take some other church's generic model, without considering whether your theology is consistent with theirs. So if you ever have a chance to be part of designing a church meeting house, ask yourself some basic questions. *Who is Sunday morning for?* Find out from your elders, *What are the high values of our church: The Lord's table? Fellowship? Baptism? Study? Preaching? Scripture reading? Congregational fellowship? Congregational singing?* Then ask, *how can our building help us to carry out our theological emphases?* Of course, worship style is also a significant consideration. But be aware that the style of worship in your church may be very different five years from now than it is today.

In this chapter, we have explored current and future worship. You might say we have considered preparing our congregation for future worship. In the next chapter, we turn our attention to preparing the worship leader.

Reflection/Application

Here is a creative project for you. Design the interior layout for a church worship center, with these functions already given: The shape of the building shell is square, and this weekend there will be one thousand committed disciples who will gather for the purpose of worship. There are no limits as to budget or space. So, design an (not necessarily *the*) ideal use for worship space, in accordance with the parameters given.

PART FOUR

LEADING IN
THE JOURNEY

CHAPTER SEVEN

BECOMING A WORSHIP LEADER

WHAT GOD IS LOOKING FOR IN A WORSHIPER

God does look for true worshipers, not just worship leaders. Jesus said that the Father is seeking those who will worship Him in spirit and in truth (John 4:23). The Bible tells us that "the eyes of the LORD range throughout the earth to strengthen those whose hearts are fully committed to him" (2 Chr 16:9). In short, if you want to be a worship leader, God's goal is for you to be a lead worshiper first. In this chapter we will explore those spiritual qualities and practical skills needed to be a successful worship leader today.

PREPARATION OF AN EFFECTIVE WORSHIP LEADER

What qualities are essential for an effective worship leader? In many ways, a worship leader needs to be more multiskilled than any other staff position in a church.[1] Let us explore the many skills necessary for success as a worship leader.

Of course, a worship leader must know music well. Actually, there are three different musical languages in which he or she must be fluent: Grand staff reading, open score reading, and chord chart reading. Printed choral and keyboard music on grand staves requires rapid note reading. Reading instrumental music from an open score requires knowledge of orchestral instruments and transposition. And working from chord charts requires having an exceptional ear and improvisational skills. Add to those three musical languages the music of other cultures and ethnic groups. There are many musical languages spoken around the world, and a worship leader should know how to acquire new musical languages as they develop.

Beyond music, a well-prepared worship leader should have a solid grasp of the Bible, especially of the theology of worship in both the Old and New Testaments. He or she must know well the development of worship in the history of the church, including the current trends in various worshiping communities today. The worship leader increasingly needs to direct many of the fine and performing arts, and needs to have both background education and current skills in them. A worship leader needs to be a team player, with a good grasp of how the programs all fit together in the overall mission of the church. And most of all, an effective worship leader must know God personally, and have a vital relationship with the Lord.

What Are Churches Looking for in Worship Leadership?

What do churches think they want in a worship leader? What do they *really* want? What do they *need?* What if they *get* what they *want?* What if they *get* what they *need?* Let me try to address these five questions.

Many churches look at the magnetic church down the street, and ask, "What do they have that we don't have?" Often, the answer is that they have a strong music and worship program. The worship leader has a charismatic persona and an enthusiasm that draws the community into the church. He or she leads the music with quality, the congregational singing with smoothness, and the big programs with flair. In some ways the music person shapes the "personality" of the congregation even more than the preaching minister does.

The church might think that they want someone like that, to make their worship service a magnet. That may be what they *think* they want. But what do they *really* want? Sometimes the cynical side of me says they want someone to take the heat for their indecision about music styles. Too often I see young Bible college students brought into a church that tells them, "We are rather traditional, but we want someone to help us move into a more contemporary worship style." Like a sacrificial lamb, that idealistic student comes into the church and does what they said they wanted, only to become the target of criticism and controversy. I understand that sometimes those young students make mistakes that a more experienced person would not make. However, sometimes elders have only a general concept about direction. They are silent when they needed to provide training and advice, and they speak up at the wrong time after the damage is already done. Then they give up on the change they thought they wanted. They thought they wanted updated music but might not have realized the cost.

What do they *need?* Many churches *think they want* a change in music, coupled with a dynamic personality. What they *really want* is someone to help them decide how to resolve their struggle over worship styles. But all the while what they *really needed* was *worship renewal!* They didn't necessarily need a change in music style, or someone with a fine personality. What they really need is to find out what worship is in the first place, and then they need somebody to help them get there. In short, they needed to experience Christ in their midst!

What happens if a church *gets* what they think they *want?* They might get the charismatic personality they thought they wanted, but they find out that the person is spiritually shallow, ambitious, and egocentric. What they *really* needed was a worship leader, not a snappy program.

What if a church *gets* what they really *need?* What if worship renewal happens? What if Christ is experienced in their midst? Unhappily, Christ may not be what many of the members *want!* (Are you staying with this so far?) True worship means life change, and life change is not what many American Christians are looking for. So when they get the very thing they need, they find that their church is experiencing difficulty. Some of the members think it's too "charismatic." Others don't like the unpredictability of the worship plan. Others are offended at the lengthy prayers, or the tearful testimonies, or the public repentance. They wanted to keep God in His comfortable box, and like the Pharisees of Jesus' day, they are offended when He doesn't fit their preconceived notions of what worship should resemble.

Pardon me if this all comes across as cynical. (I warned you at the beginning that I was a cynic!) But it is important for churches to realize that often they are asking the impossible from someone, and that there will be problems no matter who leads worship, or in what direction. It is also important for those preparing to be worship leaders to be prepared for criticism and controversy. But take heart! Jesus Himself was killed by His constituents after a three year ministry,[2] and the great apostle Paul caused riots and revivals everywhere he went. So you are in good company. Remember, our Lord told us that it was the false prophets who were well spoken of by everyone (Luke 6:26).

The Top Skills Needed in a Worship Leader

In baseball, the most valuable players are five-tool players; they can hit for power and for average, and they have a great glove and a great arm, and they have speed. On top of it all, managers are looking for men who enjoy the game and are a good influence in the clubhouse. Even on the major league level, these players are hard to find.

Churches similarly are looking for worship facilitators who are five tool players. The skills I hear most often that they are looking for are these: Music skills. People skills. Organizational skills. A heart for God. Maturity. They must have music skills and stage presence, must have people skills and be administrators, and must be theologically and biblically astute. On top of it all, they must be team players and not overshadow the other programs of the church. Such people are hard to find.

As you can see, churches are looking for people with more than just musical skills. A worship leader must work through other musicians, anyway. So having good people skills, organizational skills, and a heart for God, you can be effective in leading worship just because you know where you want the congregation to go. You may need somebody else to do the role of chief musician, but do not despair if music is your weakest area.

A Worship Leader's Job Description

Most churches seek a male[3] with a good personality who can sing well and build a team of musicians. Depending on the style of music, they would like him to play guitar well, or keyboard. Almost invariably, the worship minister is in charge of scheduling musicians, including "specials" and other presentations using the creative and performing arts. Of course, developing new talent is an implied responsibility. Beyond that, there is much flexibility as to what duties fall under the jurisdiction of the worship minister.

A full-time worship leader can expect to be busy at least three nights a week with rehearsals. If the church has several hundred members, you can expect to be busy with weddings on many Saturdays, as well as packing in rehearsals on the weekends. You will want to clarify about the church's expectations for office hours in light of all this, for the music-oriented person must keep hours more akin to a realtor than a banker.

Title of the Worship Leader

You might say that the job title itself is the church's short version of the job description. You could anticipate a very different expectation from a church that calls the position "song leader" or "choir director," compared to "worship pastor" or "fine arts director." Here is a partial list of possible titles for "the" position.

❖ Psalmist
❖ Worship Leader
❖ Chief Musician
❖ Minister of Music
❖ Worship Minister
❖ Minister of Worship
❖ Worship Pastor
❖ Pastor of Performing Arts
❖ Performing Arts Director
❖ Worship Facilitator
❖ Shepherd of Worship
   Ministries
❖ Creative Arts Staff
❖ Communication Arts
❖ Priest

❖ Father
❖ Brother / Sister
❖ Associate Minister
❖ Minister
❖ Servant Shepherd
❖ Lay Leader
❖ Liturgist
❖ Liturgy Programmer
❖ Program Director
❖ Cantor
❖ Song Leader
❖ Choir Director
❖ Song Evangelist
❖ Music Evangelist
❖ Worship Evangelist

THE WORSHIP LEADER AS PASTOR, PROPHET, AND PRIEST

The worship leader has a clear *pastoral* role with the congregation. A shepherd is to tend, bestow care, and gather the flock, and to help the flock to be fruitful and increase in number.[4] That is the role of a pastor, and it is a function that an effective worship leader must fulfill for the gathered church. You choose songs, lead in prayer and readings and other acts of worship that will help to feed the sheep, take care of the weak, tend the sick, bind up the broken, and go looking for those who have wandered away and are lost. In many ways, the worship leader is actually more of a pastor than the preaching minister is, if you take this role seriously.

Worship leading also has a certain *prophetic* role. You might be considered a church musician with a preacher's heart. As worship leader, you preach, but you use someone else's words in putting your message together (Scripture reading, words of hymns and choruses, drama, etc.). It is a more "creative" and inductive method of preaching, but it is preaching nonetheless. God may have called you to be a preacher, but not in the traditional sense of delivering sermons.

A prophet (in this sense) speaks to people on behalf of God. The function of a prophet was clear (*see* Ezekiel 33 and Jeremiah 1:7-10,17-19). He or she was to warn, to speak out to dissuade evil ways, to go where God sends, say what He says, uproot, tear down, destroy or overthrow what He does, and build and plant what the Lord says to build or plant. A prophet declares or tells forth the will and message of God, no more, no less, and nothing besides. You might say that effective worship cannot avoid prophecy forever and still be worship.

Of course, some see prophecy as a spiritual gift belonging only to the apostles' generation. For our purposes, I am using a more general application of the concept of "prophecy." There is a certain modern-day prophetic function apart from getting into the finer points of what exactly constitutes prophecy. Nonetheless, there is a strong correlation between prophecy and music, and it is appropriate to at least mention that correlation here.[5]

There is also a *priestly* function for the worship leader. If a prophet speaks to the people on God's behalf, a priest speaks to God on the people's behalf. Priests had the function of ministering before the ark, of making petition, of giving thanks, and of praising the Lord (*see* 1 Chronicles 16:4-6). Today, ALL believers are members of the priesthood, and can perform all of these functions. However, as a worship leader there is a sense in which you speak as representative for the people. For example, when leading in public prayer, you represent the prayers of others as you speak to God. You offer up a token of what others are also offering up to Him. The Psalms helped people speak to God by putting into words some common expressions and thoughts. As worship leaders and songsters, we similarly give people words to sing and ideas to express to God what they may have been feeling but couldn't articulate. You might say a worship leader helps people pray.

The Worship Leader as Producer, Arranger, Manager, and Trainer

There are four musical functions of a worship leader, which are often assumed to the point of being overlooked by both the church and the leader. Yet, these four roles are crucial for long-term success in ministry.

First, the worship leader must serve as a *Producer*. In a sense, every assembly is a production, whether it is a small group singing a spontaneous worship set, or a megachurch with lights and multimedia presentations. The more layers of production happen (larger band, more media, etc.), the more planning, coordination, and communication must take place going into it. Perhaps no church ever gets to quite the level of producing a Broadway musical each week, but with each person who is added to the production team, the worship catalyst (or an appointee on your behalf) becomes more of a producer. Therefore, a worship leader is wise to know as much as possible about computer projection software, stage lighting systems, set design, storyboards, and critical paths.

The worship leader also serves as an *Arranger*. The days of using only a hymnal for congregational singing are past in most churches. Today, many songs are mimicked by ear from a CD recording, or learned at a conference, or built from memory and a downloaded chord chart. The chief musician must be the coordinator to help each member of the worship team play with excellence, within his or her ability. Such an approach to worship music requires a sophisticated ear and advanced music arranging skills, even in a small worship team. It requires an understanding of each instrument and voice part, and often requires an ability to adjust to the skill level of the musicians or to spontaneous creativity within rehearsal or the assembly itself.

The worship leader must also serve as a *Manager*. Each member of the worship team has his or her personal calendar, and each has a skill level. For that matter, each is in a different place spiritually. Each week, the worship leader coordinates those schedules so as to put together a team that will function effectively, while giving appropriate breaks for refreshment (or discipline) and to create a strong ministry team. Such coordination requires more than just a schedule of rotation, but also involves spiritual sensitivity and uncommon people skills.

Lastly, the worship leader must serve as a *Trainer*. Arranging music and coordinating schedules will keep a team working for months or even years, but eventually more musicians and even worship leaders must be trained. Part of the job of ministry is to reproduce yourself—your spiritual walk, your skills, your thinking patterns—in others. Some training is simply *caught* as you work together, but much of it must also be purposefully *taught*, or it will not be understood. So, never lose sight of the end goal of working yourself out of a job. After all, the only guarantee about your position is that someday you will be gone.

Reflection/Application

What title would you prefer for yourself as a worship facilitator in a church? (see page 202)

In which of the following areas of skill or responsibility do you personally feel most qualified, or what sounds like the best match for how God has wired you? Check as many as apply.

❏ Pastor/shepherd
❏ Prophet/proclaimer
❏ Priest/liturgist
❏ Musician
❏ People skills
❏ Organize/administrate
❏ Heart for God
❏ Maturity
❏ Producer/Arranger
❏ Manager/Trainer

Turn the page for the next step

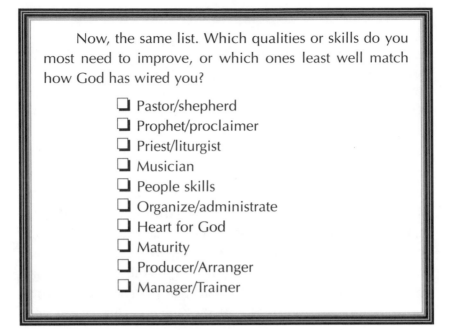

Now, the same list. Which qualities or skills do you most need to improve, or which ones least well match how God has wired you?

❏ Pastor/shepherd
❏ Prophet/proclaimer
❏ Priest/liturgist
❏ Musician
❏ People skills
❏ Organize/administrate
❏ Heart for God
❏ Maturity
❏ Producer/Arranger
❏ Manager/Trainer

A Call for Spiritual Leadership in Worship

A worship leader most effectively facilitates worship in others by being a lead worshiper. That means you must be a spiritual pilgrim yourself before you can take others on pilgrimage.

A lead worshiper must be sensitive to the Spirit of God. Too many times we worship leaders rely on music to substitute for the Spirit. Music is the sacrament of this generation of worshipers, as was said earlier.[6] We choose from our "hot list," or brainstorm on a theme, or develop a song set, and then think that worship leading is merely carrying out the plan for the congregation. Instead, we must personally hunger for and seek the Lord on a daily basis. We cannot take people where we are not willing to go ourselves. On Sundays, our job is to sense the needs and responses in the people, and to listen to the Spirit's gentle prompting. It's not all about a song list; it's all about God being among His people!

TRUE SPIRITUAL WORSHIP

Jesus said that the Father is seeking worshipers who worship "in spirit." If we can worship in spirit, then it must be possible to worship *not* in spirit, but in flesh. What does worship in the flesh look like? More importantly, what does worship in the spirit look like? Does it mean to speak in tongues? Does it mean to worship sincerely? Does it mean to worship engaging the emotions? All of the above? None of the above?

Some believers have an objective, covenantal, or even sacramental view of things of the Spirit. The Holy Spirit regenerates a person in baptism, apart from feelings or experience. The Word of God is the only tool that the Spirit uses, and so to be saturated with Scripture is equivalent to being filled with the Spirit. The Spirit did wonders in the days of the apostles, but He does not bestow such sign gifts today.

Others have a subjective, pietistic, and experiential view of things of the Spirit. The baptism of the Spirit may or may not have anything to do with water baptism. The Spirit works through continued revelation, giving the same signs and wonders and wishing to communicate as much today as He did 2000 years ago. Daily He leads in a mysterious, to some, nearly audible voice.

Because of the vast chasm between these two views of the Holy Spirit, the church may be more divided on this subject than any other. In this section, I am proposing something of a both/and approach to those different views. It may be controversial to my objective friends, but I am convinced that the Spirit works in some mysterious, indefinable, but experiential way today. I hope to present my view of how I understand His work in worship leading.

THE SPIRIT AND THE SOUL

You might say that our spirit is what makes us in the image of God. It is the deepest part of us, so deep that we have no descriptive words for it (such as we have for the soul), and it is shrouded in mystery.

Because the body houses the soul, it is easy to get the two

confused. We talk about the heart (or the bowels of compassion), or your head or brain, as if they are mechanical sources of emotion or will. The soul cannot noticeably exist without a body, but the body is not the source of the soul.

In the same way, we can easily confuse the soul and the spirit. They are both part of the "heart," and the term "heart" could apply to either spirit or soul. Because the soul houses the spirit, we can think that our intelligence, our will, or our emotions are the level on which we commune with God. However, Scripture tells us that our spirits are what testify that we are the children of God, and our spirits are what will live eternally. Your spirit is that deepest part of you that lives forever, that is the essence of your being. It is the deep that calls out to the deep of God (Ps. 42:7); it is what witnesses with God's Spirit that we are His children;[7] it is what is regenerated. We may not be able to distinguish between the soul and the spirit, but the Word of God is able to divide them and to make that distinction (Heb. 4:12; *see* also 1 Thess. 5:23).

You could depict body, soul, and spirit as three concentric circles.[8] All people are body and heart, and all hearts are soul and spirit, and all souls are mind, will, and emotions. We have been created as spiritual beings. Animals may have a "soul," in the sense that they have intellect, a will, and emotions. But humans alone have a spirit within that soul. We alone have personhood, creativity, self-awareness, and an inborn sense of eternality.

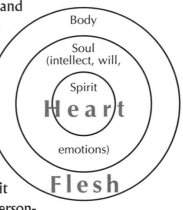

I heard it explained this way somewhere: Many of us come to Christ by being intellectually convinced about the Christian philosophy. Or perhaps empirical evidence converts our *minds* to accept Christ.

Others are won to Christ through their *wills*. When we choose to give up the personal control of our lives to the lordship of

Christ, we submit our wills to His, and our repentance marks our discipleship.

Still others come to Christ through the *emotions*. Perhaps through storytelling, a song, or a powerful drama, our emotions were moved to compassion and love for God.

In these ways, people can come to Christ through the *soul*. In fact, many churches call themselves "*soul*-winning" churches. They convert people through their intellect, their wills, or their emotions. Of course, when God has control of the soul, He gains control of the body as well. However, the soul is on that border between spirit and flesh. The flesh cannot please God (Romans 8:8), and worship that is "soulish" is not the kind that He is looking for.

Ultimately, the center of the matter is not being convinced, or being changed, or being moved. The center is being born again. We need the Holy Spirit of God to regenerate our dead spirits and give us new life. Once the Spirit has given life to our spirits, then our souls are changed, and also our bodies. Ultimately, it's a "spirit thing," not a "soul thing."

Perhaps this is splitting hairs, for God wants all of us, and any part of us without the rest is, no doubt, not a full conversion. All of your flesh—body, mind, will, emotions—must be submitted to the lordship of Christ. Yet, there are subtle but significant differences that bear explanation.

Talents or Spiritual Gifts?

God gives all people natural gifts. Even the unconverted are given certain aptitudes and talents which affect their bodies and their souls (mind, will, and emotions). Music is one of those natural gifts, for it is an emotional expression of the soul.

But *spiritual* gifts are only given to those who are born again of the water and of the Spirit. These gifts are planted into our spirits by the "supernatural" work of God (in contrast to the "natural" gifts, which also come from Him).

How Does That Affect Spiritual Worship?

Now, about worship: I used to think that worship "in spirit and in truth" was roughly equivalent to worship "in emotion and in doctrine." Painting in very broad strokes, that may be the case. But more recently I am seeing that "in spirit" might go deeper to our center than "in emotion," which is to say "in soul."

We can easily worship in "soul" and in truth, rather than in spirit. Here are some symptoms of "soulish" worship: Soulish worship might be *musically-dependent* worship, since music is a soul gift. But if we need music in order to experience the presence of God, we may have simply fallen prey to musical idolatry, reaching people on an *emotional* level, but not a spiritual one.[9]

"Soulish" worship might be *lesson-centered*, presented through thematically-driven creative education. The elements of the assembly make sense to the *mind*, but are not necessarily dwelling on that somehow-deeper plane. "Soulish" worship might even be *behavior-centered*, aimed at the will, calling for conviction and repentance. But spiritual worship must go deeper to be truly acceptable to God.

When we live spiritually, we live in constant communication with God's Spirit, and we are guided by Him, in step with Him, led by Him, and walking in Him. So, the Spirit uses Scripture (cp. Eph. 5:18 with Col. 3:15) but is not limited to Bible study. If we are saturated with Scripture, we have given our spirits a vocabulary with which God can speak to us and a measure by which to test the spirits. He also prompts (*see* Acts 8:26-29), checks (*see* Acts 16:6,7), empowers (*see* 1 Cor. 5:4), and speaks to our spirits.

When we live in our souls, we hear from ourselves, that is, our flesh, and yield the fruit of the fleshly life. When our worship is "soulish," our lifestyle is marked by striving, frustration, burnout, self-promotion, selfish ambition, shallowness, anxiety about money, and a need to control.[10] We are marked by the fruit described in Galatians 5:13-21, which includes a legalistic spirit, divisiveness, discord, jealousy, selfish ambition, dissensions, factions, and envy, as well as more obvious sins of immorality.

On the other hand, when our lives are in step with the Spirit, our lives are marked by everyday miracles of Divine providence. We have overwhelming peace and contentment, freshness, a desire to promote the life and ministry of others, humility, depth, trust in God's adequate provision, and letting go and letting God do His thing.[11] The fruit of our lives is love, joy, peace, patience, kindness, goodness, faithfulness, gentleness, and self-control (Gal. 5:22-23).

Which list best describes you? If you are walking in the Spirit, you may even be mistaken for a drunkard at times, because you are no longer concerned about protecting your carefully-honed dignity.[12] Somehow, being filled with the Spirit is experiential, more than just intellectual!

In this chapter, we have covered the preparation for a worship leader. In the next chapter, we will pursue this more thoroughly from a practical level.

Reflection/Application

In your opinion, how can a worship leader tell whether he or she is planning or leading worship "in the flesh"? How does this differ from planning or leading "in the Spirit," on a practical level? Can you tell from looking at the outside? Can you tell in your own heart?

CHAPTER EIGHT

Practical How-To's

Keys to Effective Planning and Leading

\

This book started with practical assessment of your church and then gave general principles for rethinking your assembly. Here it provides a practical guide for those who regularly plan and lead worship in the assembly.

Part One: Purposeful Planning

Before you get out there in front of the congregation and start leading in worship, you must have a clear plan that is balanced, practical, wise, and spiritual. In this chapter, we will deal with how to go about crafting a careful plan that will glorify God, edify the saints, and win the lost. Such noble goals must involve a noble plan that has been shrewdly, innocently prayed over and crafted.

The Advantages of "Purposeful" Flowing Worship

Remember the "colors" of worship, described in chapter two? The last color bar on p. 46 was the color white. When the three primary colors of light are combined, they create white light. So, when a worship planner purposely chooses to borrow from different worship traditions or approaches, the worship is a purposeful blend.

For each different worship tradition, there is a corresponding system for planning, and there are advantages and disadvantages to each. For example, the liturgical tradition follows the church calendar. Following the calendar saves planning time, preserves organized readings, and brings us back to the Christ Event every year, so that we don't lose our balance. On the other hand, there are disadvantages to liturgical worship. It loses spontaneity, it can fall prey to dry irrelevance, and you can fall into a rut.

What I advocate often is to freely borrow from every tradition that is of relevance to your congregation. Constantly read and stretch your understanding of worship. If you do, your journey can be a continual pilgrimage, and you can find true freedom.[1]

Step One: Gathering a Worship Programming Team

Your first step is to gather a team of people to help in planning assemblies. A group of up to six or eight people can greatly help to spread the work, share the ministry, model unity, increase accountability, and improve creativity. All of us go through dry times, and a group will help you to ride through it. Hopefully, all eight of you will not be dry at the same time!

Who should be a member of your team? There is no standard formula. Jesus prayed all night before choosing the twelve, and they were an unlikely combination of men. Yet, they were the ones the Father revealed for Jesus to choose. Nonetheless, consider having someone who represents these functions on your team: the vocalists; the instrumentalists; the sound, light, and video technicians; the drama team; the elders; the preaching minister; the youth; and the elderly. You might consider having some "specialists" on your team: someone who knows the Bible well, someone who focuses on choir music, on hymnals, on new choruses, on classic choruses, on presentation music, and on drama scripts. You might also try to create a set of members who will rotate the responsibility of up-front leadership, even as they plan as a group.

How often should the group meet? Again, there is no set formula. I've tried many different plans over the years, which change with the needs of the church and the makeup of the group. You can meet once a month, and plan or assign duties many weeks in advance. Or, you can meet every week, and work just a few weeks in advance. You can combine the planning with the rehearsing, if your worship team musicians are a small enough group.

Step Two: Conducting the Meetings

How do you actually conduct the planning meetings? Here's my personal advice as to what works best for me, but different leaders work different ways: Begin with knowing the "center" of your worship style,[2] so that your team doesn't veer from its basic vision. It is easier than you would think to forget that you are supposed to be seeker-centered, or mostly traditional, or only semi-thematically driven. Especially if the elders have determined those priorities, you want to be sure everyone understands and is in agreement with the "color" and balance of the worship.

The meeting should consist of a combination of brainstorming for a future service, and of crafting the plan for an already-roughed-in assembly plan. For the future service plan, do some brainstorming on songs, Scripture, presentation music, dramas, and other components that will enhance the theme or advance the worship. The only rule for the brainstorm session is that no critical comment is allowed, or it will immediately dry up all creativity. My advice is that you not try to polish the list, but that you then move on to assign the critical assessment and polishing to one person. That person takes the list home, and works to eliminate components and craft a roughed-in service plan. The group then hears the plan presented, and gives further support and comment. After that second brainstorm session, someone again takes the service to hone it, with transitions, key changes, lighting cues, and so forth added in. By the third level of planning as a group, the committee's work is to help refine the details or add sparks of creativity to the plan.

Step Three: Thinking in "Worship Sets"

When planning the congregational participation for the assembly, it is helpful to think in terms of "worship sets." These are blocks of activities[3] that function as "miniservices." These sets are then put together like Lego™ blocks to fit together as a larger unit. To do worship set planning,[4] it is wise to start with a blank (or nearly-blank) piece of paper, perhaps with a template of components.

A worship set could be as short as one transition (word of introduction, Scripture reading or prayer) that leads into a song. It could be as long as 8-10 songs strung together in a long medley that flows seamlessly without endings and startups. Most sets are made up of 2-3 songs, with some unifying event tying them together. That unifying event could be a drama, a transition, or a song. In any case, the components all fit together to form something of a unit that can stand on its own.

Here are some templates that have helped us over the years: You can construct your worship in three sets: Praise, Theme, and Worship.[5] Or, if you are less thematically driven, your three sets could be Invitation, Celebration, and Consecration.[6] For many churches, it works well to plan using four sets, of Ingathering, Word, Table, and Sending Forth.[7] A variation of that pattern found in many Christian churches is Worship, Table, Word, and Response.[8] Many churches seem to have time for only two sets, which might be Praise and Table.[9] Even the most traditional of evangelical churches can structure with one opening worship set before the static events.[10] It may help you to construct your plans by using one of these templates.

Each set should have one designated leader to oversee its rehearsal and to maintain the congregation during its execution. The designated leader can, of course, be the same person who always leads worship. But you can also rotate leaders, not just

Sunday to Sunday, but from set to set. That person will generally sing the lead part and be in charge of watching the congregation. The leader will also have the authority to change the set at certain predetermined junctions.[11] One person decides which way to go at that junction, and everyone follows.

Step Four: Developing a Sense of "Flow"

Some song services are choppy. They are a series of songs and (perhaps) other events, but something seems to be lacking. As happens when you engage the clutch on a car while in the wrong gear, the service seems to lurch forward, then jerk to a stop, then jump forward again throughout the assembly.

Let's imagine that you have brainstormed a list of 30 songs that might be appropriate for use in a worship set. How do you go from having a song list that you brainstormed to put together, to craft a worship assembly with a sense of flow to it? Here are seven suggestions to help with that. You might consider this to be a sevenfold grid through which to filter your song service before making final preparations. Use these filters to decide which songs or events to cut, or what order to put them in, or how to lead from one song or event to another. This is the crafting process in worship planning that makes the difference between a series of disconnected events and a purposeful, smooth-flowing service.

1. FRESHNESS. Use the **peak of freshness** of every song in your set. First, determine the familiar/unfamiliar ratio of the songs in the set.[12] For most worship settings,[13] about 90% of your choices should already be familiar to the congregation. Then, further determine how to make each song "fresh" to the congregation. Some songs are overly familiar to the point of being stale. Others are too new for people to sing along well yet. There are many ways to restore freshness to an old song: change some musical aspect of it,[14] share an insight to put it into a new context,[15] or in some other way add to the spirit and the understanding of people's singing. There are also several ways to speed a new song to its peak of freshness: use it

in presentation format first,[16] provide clear helps to eliminate confusion,[17] or in some other way help people become familiar and comfortable with the song. You want them to get beyond the mechanics of how the tune goes or of learning what the words are, and start to focus on the message of the song.

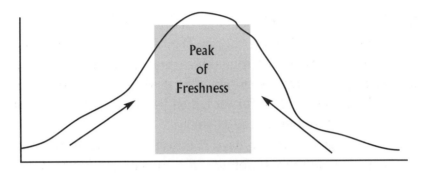

2. TRANSITIONS. Transitions are often the difference between a pleasant song set and a life-changing worship moment. If the songs in a worship set are bricks, transitions are the mortar that strengthens the wall. A brick wall is not strong without mortar to hold the bricks together. Transitions can be musical or verbal, and they must be spiritual, sensitive, and skillful. **Musical transitions** can keep the "mood" from breaking by smoothly moving from one song to the next.[18] **Verbal transitions** can likewise help the congregation sing with spirit and understanding. In most American churches,

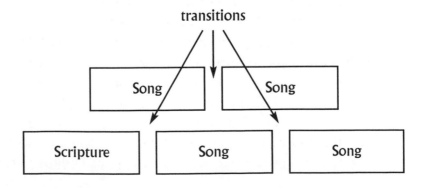

any service can tolerate one "worship focus," which serves as a short (less than five minute) teaching time to guide the insights and expressions of the congregation. A few songs will also require some explanations of how the "mechanics" of the song work.[19] Speak little, but always toward increasing the understanding of the worshiper.

3. MOOD. Be aware of **emotional levels** of excitement. As you structure your song list, run them through the filter of mood. Carefully pace the congregation through smooth shifts in levels of excitement.[20] As explained elsewhere, many churches begin with songs that are engaging and fast. A celebrative atmosphere of praise invites involvement and helps to break down self-conscious inhibitions.[21] After some time of high energy, there is a transition that moves to reflective, intimate worship. In quiet worship, people pray, adore, and consecrate themselves to the Lord. In some ways, the prayer of consecration is the highest act of worship, so you must approach this time with sensitivity. However, usually it is not good to leave them there. We want to close out our time with hope and joy again. After people have been experiencing introspective confession and intimate adoration, be especially careful about how you bring them back out. When you are transitioning from quiet to celebrative, be sure they are fully motivated and ready to celebrate. It is like taking away someone's coat on a cold day if you sing cheerful songs to a heart that is still heavy (Proverbs 25:20).

Emotional levels

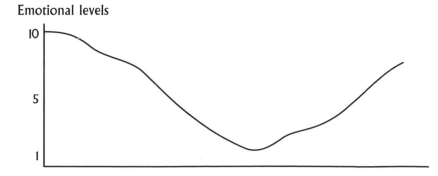

4. EXHORTATION TO PRAYER. This filter discerns **whom you address** in song. In particular, the question is whether God is addressed in the second person (Thou or You) or the third person (Him or He). Most churches try to structure their worship sets starting with exhorting one another to praise,[22] and then shift to direct expressions of prayer.[23] Once you have taken people into a place of prayer, addressing God directly, be careful to avoid a sudden shift back to exhortation again, even if the emotion and the musical elements feel right. A sensitive worshiper will feel jerked from intimate communion to have to sing to people again.[24]

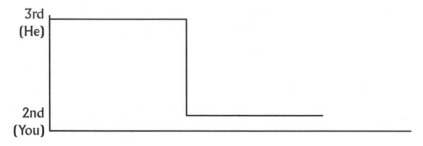

5. CORPORATE TO PERSONAL. This filter is similar to the last, but it discerns **who is singing**. In particular, it clarifies whether the singer is singular in number (I or me) or plural (we or us). For most churches,[25] it seems to work best to use a structure that begins with group singing and carefully moves to intimate worship. First, people are more self-conscious, and so we sing to one another songs of ingathering, inviting each other to come and worship. Then together we declare the majesty of God. But eventually, most of your worshipers will be ready to speak directly and personally with the Lord, doing personal business with God.[26] As with the last filter, be careful to be gentle when leading the group back from this place of personal intimacy and back to community.

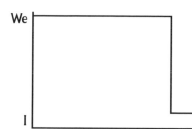

6. THE MOMENT. In the first chapter, we discussed "worship moments." Be aware that some people in your church may be having one of those moments in any given service. Don't manipulate them with music and psychology, but set the table attractively for the meal. Then aim for one song, or one insight to be the **central focus** of your time together. The entire set does not need to be built around a central theme in order to accomplish such a moment,[27] but the pacing and structure of the immediate context should be crafted to frame the focus and allow for people to linger in an extended moment of glimpsing eternity. Sometimes this moment could be the Lord's Supper, as you highlight a new facet of the jewel that is the Feast. Other times, it could be that you started with ingathering exhortation, moved to uninhibited exaltation, and then transitioned down to intimate adoration. On the way, you provided a new insight to bring worshipers to a new level in their walk with God. A word of warning: aim for only one central focus in any given assembly.[28] And if you have a great moment planned, but God seems to be doing a work among people before you get there, be willing to linger where you are

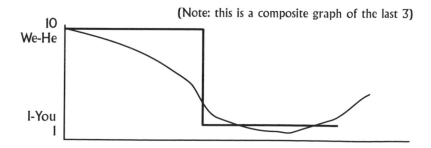

(Note: this is a composite graph of the last 3)

and let that become the central moment for the morning, rather than the extended one you had planned.[29]

7. BALANCE OF GENRE. It is good to determine the **mix of song styles** for your church before you start the selections for a particular assembly. That keeps you from choosing all of your own favorite songs, or those of your planning team. For our purposes, I like to categorize songs in four ways: hymns,[30] gospel songs,[31] "classic" choruses,[32] and new songs.[33] Some churches might choose equal balance of the four categories each week. Others might use five or six new choruses, with maybe one song from each of the other three categories. Still others might use almost exclusively one of the four categories, with occasional use of one of the others. Find the right balance for your church, and then use your rule of thumb as one of the grids through which you filter your song selection.

Step Five: Specific Components to Consider

A. The Call to Worship

The opening activity in the assembly is important. It will set the tone for the assembly with reverent worship, celebrative praise, spiritual truth, joyous participation, or trying to overcome self-conscious inhibitions. It will also imply or state the theme and purpose for the assembly.

Many churches open the same way every week. Others change the opening, based on the theme or purpose of the gathering that week. Some open with a spoken welcome and invitation to join in worship. Others open with a Scripture statement (such as, "The Lord is in His holy temple. Let all the earth keep silence before Him.") or Psalm reading. Many open with an upbeat song that invites active participation. Many others open with instrumental music, whether as prelude or as the first act of worship. The style of music itself will set the tone. Many churches today use a loop of slides with announcements and a relatively quiet music CD before and into the beginning of the service. Some will start the service with some performance music, usually a vocal solo, choral piece, or instrumental offering.

If you begin with a quiet, prayerful song or reading, be careful how you come out of it. If you begin with upbeat, celebrative music, be careful about what happens right before you start it.

B. Emphasizing Different Components of the Assembly

Every assembly cannot emphasize the same thing, or we risk imbalance at ignoring others. Some churches emphasize testimonies, but don't have much time for prayer. Others include the Lord's Supper, but emphasize only the personal inspection facet, and ignore communal aspects of the Table. Others make it their practice to deemphasize the offering, but they miss the blessing of occasionally treating offering as a public act of joyful sacrifice.

Over the years, some of these elements of the assembly have formed a kind of mental checklist for me. I revisit the list on occasion to see if we have preserved balance by placing an extra emphasis on a given component lately. I share it with you, with the hope that it will spur new acts of joyful celebration as your congregation comes to new aspects of balance. On any given week you can emphasize one or more of the following:

1. **Expressiveness.** Emphasize postures and encourage participation. Increase your congregation's postural and expressive vocabulary.
2. **Testimonies.** Everyone comes with a story to tell. Some are of a level to be told to close friends. But some are the kind that would greatly edify the whole church.
3. **Performance.** Excellence in presentation music to proclaim truth. Have members or guests share lessons or testimonies in the form of song.
4. **Drama.** Let a prepared drama serve as a powerful illustration. This can be done through pre-recorded video or live, and can be folded into the sermon or stand alone.
5. **Personal sharing.** We find ways to hear and meet personal needs. Usually, the grieving or suffering are ministered to pri-

vately, but occasionally the whole church needs to know, and to spring into action.

6. **Giving**. Emphasize some aspect of offering and stewardship. Let the church know the hilarity of generosity and offering.

7. **Prayer**. Be a house of prayer, giving special attention to extended time. Take a new approach to the prayer, with a specific topic, or in different groupings.

8. **The worldwide church**. Emphasize missions, and the Persecuted church. Remind ourselves of living martyrs. Hear from some of your congregation's links around the world.

9. **Scripture**. Take extended reading time to let God speak. In a special and creative way, let people hear God speak for Himself.

10. **Silence**. Give people time to listen and interact, without doing. After Scripture reading or some other act, have purposeful silence.

11. **Confession**. Provide a means for individuals to publicly or privately repent. Sometimes an "altar call," and sometimes through emphasizing a prayer and reconciliation room, give them a chance to do business with God.

12. **The Table**. Teach a different aspect and take it differently. Whatever your tradition has been, explore a new facet of meaning as you symbolize the Meal in a new way.

13. **Children**. Find ways to highlight and bless the children among you. Let the adults humble themselves and sing the children's songs, or hear the little ones as they sing.

14. *A cappella*. Highlight the congregational choir. The term *a cappella* means, "of the chapel." Vocal singing is supposed to be the central focus of our praise.

C. Planning around a Theme

Many churches like to organize their assembly around a particular theme. Particularly in outreach-oriented churches, it is popular to center every activity within the assembly to advance or highlight a central theme. Here is some practical advice on how to weave a theme through the worship service.

Work with the sermon, if possible. Usually, that theme is the message topic.[34] But if you know the message outline, be careful not to steal the thunder of the message. You want the song service to whet the appetite, and to set the table, but let the spoken teaching be the meal. You can think of the song service as a setting for the jewel. The idea is not to draw attention to the prongs in the head that holds the jewel, but to make the jewel all the more beautiful by bringing it forward and highlighting it. If you are the worship leader, you are most likely not designated to also be the primary teacher, so know your place and work within your anointing.

Another bit of practical advice. In your planning, know how the preacher wants to start and end his message. If you finish your time with quiet, contemplative stillness, and he planned to open with a couple of jokes, you are setting him up to look spiritually insensitive. He will have to do his own improvised transition. On the other hand, it might also be possible to finish your time so exuberantly that he appears boring if he starts off low key. So try to match the mood at the beginning of his message, and have the theme flow smoothly into his speaking. Likewise, he should communicate with you about how he wants to end the message,[35] so you can keep the service moving forward with the next activity.

Whatever else you do with the central message of the day, remember that your role is to lead people in worship. Therefore, reflect every theme through the lens of worship. Most themes will fit into worship quite well,[36] for all great doctrine is worship material when it is spoken back to God.[37] For that matter, all worship is extremely practical application of any given topic, especially when you consider that worship is a lifestyle. So we study a topic, and then we say it back to God, and then we pledge our lives to live righteously, and we eat the Feast with new understanding.

A word of warning: It is easy, when planning the worship around a central theme, to become so theme-oriented that you forget to worship. This is what I referred to earlier when I wrote about the dangers of creative education. In most brainstorming groups that I have led, the first inclination of the group is to start thinking of every song that has the stated theme in it, rather than seeing the bigger picture of worship. When the programming is done, it more resembles a series of events designed to teach a lesson than an act of liturgy.

Now a word of advice: Use creativity in your planning. When your group gets together, think outside of the box. Remember, worship moments happen when creativity brings us to a new insight into the nature of God. But while being creative, be sure to stay within biblical and cultural confines. In other words, do not cross scriptural principles in order to create a good moment, and do not stretch the congregation so far that it offends or distracts them. Novelty without good communication and planning is irritating chaos. That being said, I encourage you to change the order of service to fit the needs of the moment, and to add new musical elements to generate fresh experiences for worshipers.

Last pieces of advice: Remember in the midst of worship planning to get your eyes off of yourself and prepare by worshiping God personally.[38] Prepare completely in advance, working through as many of the details as possible.[39] Notify musicians of your plans and work within their comfort zone.[40] Always work under the elders and preacher.[41] And lastly, don't get too radical and DON'T CHANGE THINGS TOO QUICKLY! Preserving traditions has its good points!

PART TWO: PRACTICAL LEADERSHIP TIPS

Every person who is in a position of leading worship is different and must find his or her own style and public personality. Personality and taste should be a reflection of how God made you, rather than how someone taught you. What follows is at best practical advice. You can take into consideration how you might apply the principles. The book has been becoming increasingly practical up to this point. Now it may become so practical as not to be applicable! I pray that will not be the case for you.

Up to this point, we have been so focused on the word "worship" that we have not spent much time talking about "leadership." Jesus was clear about the idea of leadership. If you want to be a leader, then be a servant. I used to think that meant if I serve now, some day I will be asked to be a leader. But now I think Jesus was teaching that the only leader that exists is one who serves. We never graduate from the school of humility or the institute of servanthood. You are up front to serve the congregation. You do that by making them confident enough to sing out, un-self-conscious enough to seek the Lord, and swept up to the heavenlies so as to join Him there. You sacrifice your own taste and some of your own focus on worship, so that you dedicate part of your brain to be aware of the congregation and how you can best help them. This is not an hour for impressing people with your musicianship or your personality, but an hour to serve in whatever way the Lord calls you to serve.

Tip One: Use the Isos Principle

I understand that music therapists are trained to try to match the emotions of the patients, and then perhaps to affect their mood by bringing their emotions to a new place. The art of matching a patient's emotions is called "Isos" (Greek for "same"). When you are planning and leading worship, don't rudely insist on having a congregation be where you are emotionally. Your job is to join them where most of them are, and then gently lead them to the place you want them to be.

Tip Two: Beware the Wall-o'-Sound!

Some worship leaders have a philosophy that allows most anyone to participate during the worship. They may provide percussion instruments and banners for worshipers to use, or even allow anyone who wishes to bring pitched instruments to play along with the worship team.[42]

Most evangelical churches, however, have only the musicians "up front" do the playing. If your worship team serves as the worship leading group, you should be aware of the "100% Rule," taught by the Maranatha! Praise workshops. The rule says this: if you play and sing by yourself, you alone will generate 100% of the musical activity. When you add a second instrument to the mix, you should not exceed the total amount of busyness in the sound. That means that each of you should leave room for the other. Each might contribute 50% of the total notes, but it still adds up to 100% total. Of course, if you have three rhythm guitars, an electric lead, two keyboards, a bass, a drum set and auxiliary percussionist, plus 8 vocalists, everyone is going to have to be very selective, or it will create what we call at our church the Wall-o'-Sound. When the Wall-o'-Sound happens, no one in the congregation can tell where the melody is, or what the words are, because there are so many layers of busy music all happening at the same time. There is only one dynamic: LOUD! And only one mood: overwhelmed.

Remember, it is the role of everyone on the worship team to serve the congregation. They serve by providing music to support and give confidence and emotion to the congregational singing. If the team becomes a distraction, whether by wrong notes, by too much activity, or by beautiful but performance-oriented renditions, the congregational choir has been harmed, and the very goal of the singing time has been undermined. Serve the congregation!

Tip Three: Do the Mechanics, Monitoring, and Maintenance

What is it that makes someone a worship leader, rather than just a song leader? Some of the difference is found in these three words: mechanics, monitoring, and maintenance. A song leader might give attention to the smooth presentation of a song or a song set, but a worship leader gives attention to the congregation's participation and understanding. The song leader might focus on the instrumentalists and vocalists, but the worship leader is watching the congregation. A song leader might watch the words and the music, but a worship leader has memorized and internalized the words, and watches the reaction of the worshipers. In short, a worship leader knows when to explain the mechanics of a song to the congregation, and monitors the response of the congregation to know when and how to maintain their participation and understanding.

Mechanics

Sometimes the congregation needs to be told the mechanics of how an activity might take place. In effect, they need to know the ground rules, or to be instructed on how to participate intelligently. They need to have inside information, so that they can truly be a part of the worship activity. Now, often a song is simply sung, and enough people know what to do that it happens spontaneously. But the wise worship leader knows when to anticipate that an activity might be confusing to people and what words might be helpful in advance. These I call "mechanics." Mechanics can get in the way, they can interrupt the sense of flow, and they can be distracting; so they should only be used a few times during the course of an assembly. Yet a few words carefully and succinctly worded can make a great difference in the zeal of a congregation.

Monitoring

Monitoring is also essential for the true worship leader. Many song leaders think that choosing the right song is sufficient; if the people like it, they will surely join in and sing with spirit and with mind. But a watchful worship leader is constantly monitoring the congregation with spiritual discernment. He or she is watching to sense whether or not true spiritual worship is taking place. Sometimes, people are swept up and positively responding to a particular song, or to the refrain of a song. And sometimes the worship leader notices that there is confusion or lack of participation. A worship leader understands people and knows that you don't always get what you expect from them; you only get what you inspect.

Maintenance

Wise worship leaders then know what to do about what the monitored feedback tells them. They are ready with brief words of exhortation, explanation, or encouragement, even while the song is going on. They maintain the understanding by quoting Scripture to remind the congregation of why and what they are singing. The goal is always to sing with the spirit and with understanding. I recommend that at least two or three significant insights would be ready in the heart of every worship leader for every song. You should know what Scriptures the songs you sing are based from, and you should have enough background material gleaned in preparation for the assembly that any of it could be used, but 90% of it will not be.

Tip Four: What to Do If People Don't Sing

Over the years, I have heard of five reasons for why a person does not sing in church. In my opinion, a person not singing is a symptom of a greater disease inside. Here are those five reasons, and some argument against each.

First, there is **no joy in the person's life**. James 5:13 says that if we have joy, *"let him sing."* "Let him" is a third person imperative; that means it is a command, although we cannot express it well in English. James says, "Is anyone merry? Him sing!" It is not a suggestion, not an invitation; it is a command. So if there is no joy in your life, you are exempt. Otherwise, you sing!

Second, there may be **bitterness in a person's life**. When bitterness reigns, there is no interest in merriment. In fact, the happy songs of others only serve as an irritant, like vinegar on soda or taking away someone's coat on a cold day (Prov. 25:20). Certainly, temporary setbacks can occur that get us down and cause our eyes to turn from seeing Jesus. But we need to not let ourselves stay down as we seek the Lord and receive His healing.

One of the sources of bitterness is sometimes the "worship leader" himself. For one reason or other, he or she has alienated the person, and they simply don't want to follow what is suggested by the leader. Perhaps it is poor musicianship, spiritual shallowness, not matching the person's current mood, offensive words or actions, some personal hurt, or a myriad other reasons why you just don't want to submit to the present leadership.

I remember one chapel service for me: I had just been memorizing Hebrews 13:15-16, and had written it down on a notecard that morning. As I came into the service, something about the song selection or the immaturity of the leaders caused me to want to fold my arms and sort of scowl at the people up front. Then the Lord reminded me of the very passage I was supposedly meditating on that day: *"a sacrifice of praise, the fruit of lips that confess the name of Jesus."* I realized that a sacrifice by nature is costly and not something that is naturally fun for my flesh to give. And the very sacrifice that I am to offer is lips that confess Jesus. I'm happy to say that, though it was a continuous struggle with my flesh that day, I obeyed God's command and offered a joyful sacrifice of praise that morning, and God blessed me for it.

Third, a person may feel **self-conscious about his or her voice**. Perhaps we have been ridiculed in school or by a trusted friend, and we are embarrassed by our own singing voice.

However, if you think about it, that is really pride that is keeping you from singing. David was willing to make himself quite undignified for the sake of his God (2 Sam. 6:22)! Are you not willing to do the same?

One of the most touching experiences I have had while singing in a congregation was when I sat in front of a dear brother in the Lord one Sunday. He was well-known for being "tone deaf," and I had heard him being razzed by other men from the church. When I sat in front of him, I saw why they pointed him out. Here sat Tony, singing out loudly, way off key. We were singing "Jesus Loves Me," and he was belting it out with childlike unselfconsciousness. My eyes welled up with tears at this example of one who was willing to be a fool for his Lord. That we all might learn from his example and get over our own need for reputation and simply offer to God our best. Remember, Scripture says to make a joyful noise unto the Lord, not just a beautiful song!

In fact, early philosophers and church fathers were suspicious of those who sang too beautifully! There are several writings against those who smooth their voices like those in the theatre, or those who play instruments with too many strings, or those who play too fast, so as to draw attention to the technique, as if music were a means of competition. I wonder why no one voices complaints like that in the church anymore? Could it be that we have lost our sense of balance, emphasizing excellence but forgetting humility?

On a side note, one of the most common words for praise in the Old Testament is *shabach*, which means to shout or address the Lord in a loud tone. Another word, *gil*, represents a wild, ecstatic dance before the Lord. Jesus Himself is described as having called out to God with a loud voice and many tears (Heb. 5:7). Do you ever use a loud voice? We are encouraged many times in Scripture to "call upon" the name of the Lord. So, do we? Is there ever a place in our worship practice to be loud and boisterous, and to give the same kind of enthusiastic response to God as we have for our favorite sports team? He has certainly done greater things than any sports heroes have!

Fourth, a person **who is not a Christian has reason not to sing**. If you are not a citizen of Zion, you do not really understand the songs of Zion. So you may hold off on singing until you have finished your quest. However, know that it is God's will for you to come to repentance (2 Pet. 3:9), and having come to Christ, to sing to Him (Eph. 5:19; Col. 3:16)!

Fifth and last, some people simply **prefer to listen**. My grandmother was one of those people in her later years. She said, "I have sung for 50 years, and now I just like to sit back and listen while the others carry the tune." That is certainly understandable, and is appropriate for one who has earned the rest. But by and large, we should take seriously our Lord's command to sing a new song to the Lord. Worship is not a passive verb in Scripture; it is only an active one: *praise* the Lord! (Not, "let the Lord be praised!")

When I visited a monastery a while back, I learned some important lessons from the brothers there about community

singing. First of all, each member of the community is seen as having a responsibility to the others to help carry the load. They take
the principle of sharing seriously. Each member finds his or her
own voice—a straight tone, without vibrato or stylistic flair—and
blends it with the rest. There is no room for a person singing too
softly, and no room for someone to stand out above the others.
We are all equal in this work of worship in song.

Also, all of the members of the community in that
monastery took turns being the "soloists," whether they had voices for it or not. The work of the two soloists was to provide the
pitch for the chanting of the rest. The voices provide the introductory line to start the group, and sometimes take turns in a call-
and-response fashion with the rest of the group in the responsive
psalmody. Theirs is an act of service, not of show.

TIP FIVE: PRINCIPLES FOR FACILITATING PARTICIPATION

A real challenge as a worship leader is motivating people to
follow where you want them to go without making them feel
manipulated. Here are some practical pointers on how to help
encourage people to participate with you in worship.

Scolding, belittling, or in some way judging might get results,
but it makes people feel like they have been manipulated. Many of
us have heard what Larry Bryant used to call The Christian Game:
"Good morning. (*pause, little response*). Oh, come on now. You can
do better than that. Good MOR-ning! (*murmured response*). Well, that
was better. But let me see a smile this time. GOOD MOR-ning!!
(*irritated shouts of reply*)."

How do you motivate a response, then? First, prayerfully try
to understand their side. Communicate where you think they are,
with an empathetic statement, such as: *"For many of us, this has been
a hard week."* Then, follow up that sentence by trying to get them
over to join you on your side. Use words like *we* and *us*, and invite
them, don't force them. *"We want to"* or *"I'd like to ask (invite, welcome)
you"* is received better than *"Everybody clap your hands."* (*or dance!*)

The other major factor in inviting participation is to give clear directions and boundaries. Explain the reason for what you are asking them to do. *"We'll be singing this several times through, so you can reflect on the meaning"* helps them understand the *why* behind the *what*. If you don't have a printed song list, for example, it helps to mention how long you expect to have them sing: *"We're going to be singing some songs together for the next twenty minutes. The words will be projected on the screen, or you can find them in your hymnal by noting the numbers in your program."* Talk them through the unfamiliar, and they will be more willing to join you there. *"In just a moment, we are going to ask for your response"* helps people to get set for it.

Lastly, it is essential that you aim for the newcomers in your explanations. This helps to make the first-time guests feel more comfortable, and it subtly reminds all of the members to join you in welcoming outsiders. Have no rote rituals, where everyone knows what to do before it happens.[43] For example, if you stand for Scripture reading, explain why on a regular basis: *"Let's stand together in respect for the reading of the Word of God."* Use no inside information, such as slogans and acronyms that need explaining, and do not speak in "Christianese" jargon. *"After the Invocation, all Inquirers are invited to go to the Chancel behind the Altar to receive the Ministry of the Second Work of Grace found in the Baptism of the Holy Ghost and manifested in Glossolalia and other Charismatic gifts."* Address everyone as if there for the first time. *"In a moment, our servers will be passing trays down the rows; if you are a Christian, we invite you to break off a piece of the bread and take a cup, and spend some time in reflection to eat and drink."*

Part Three: The Role of the Holy Spirit in Worship

What role does the Holy Spirit have in our assembly? First, He has provided the talent and gifts for the work, and brought the people together that He desires to do the work (*see* Exod. 4:10-17;

Acts 7:22). He has custom-built you, and each person in your congregation, to work together as His own Body (*see* 1 Cor. 12).

He is also in control, whether we work with Him or not! (*See* Acts 17:26.) He has already brought together a unique set of needs and victories to your assembly. Your job is to give opportunity for expression to it all.

Furthermore, He is guiding the church and each of its members. He makes His will known through checking our movement (*see* Acts 16:6,7), giving dreams, interpretations, words of revelation or instruction or prophecy or tongues (*see* 1 Cor. 14:26). Sometimes the leaders sense what seems good to the Holy Spirit and to them, and they make a decision accordingly (*see* Acts 15:13).

He also works wonders in our midst, at least on occasion. Jesus left the wilderness in the "power" of the Spirit (*see* Luke 4:14). The Spirit interprets our prayers according to the Father's will (*see* Rom. 8:26,27). The power of the Lord Jesus is (or at least can be, depending on how you read it) among us when we gather (*see* 1 Cor. 5:4).

Jesus said that His disciples need not worry in advance about what to say when they are brought before the authorities, for it would be given to them at the right time just what to say (Matt. 10:19-20; Luke 21:13-15). That advice may or may not be for us today (God is not necessarily dishonored by planning in advance!), but we can see His words fulfilled when Stephen stood before the council in Acts 6:15.

How does a worship leader, or a worship team member, go about planning and leading worship spiritually? First of all, the *worship leader* must be a *lead worshiper*, someone who models being a spiritual pilgrim. A lead worshiper must be walking in the Spirit, filled with the Spirit, led by the Spirit, and sensitive to the Spirit of God.

Planning in the Spirit

In the programming stage, we also need to be walking in step with the Spirit, reading daily the Scriptures, living holy lives, and hearing from God regularly. When the planning meeting begins, it should be done with earnest prayer, seeking God's guidance. In the process of brainstorming and planning details, care should be given to spiritually discern whether this is a creative fleshly idea or a godly one. The flesh is contrary to the Spirit (*see* Gal. 5:17), so spiritual discernment is essential. But it is a very difficult process, because the heart is deceitful (*see* Jer. 17:9), and we can push an idea that excites us for selfish reasons. We can be convinced that our ways are pure, but the Lord weighs the heart (Prov. 21:2), and sometimes the Spirit whispers while the flesh shouts. Carefully ask what feels "right" and is reasonable (*see* 1 Cor. 14:15). The Holy Spirit can speak and lead months in advance, just as well as He can at the moment—and it causes others much less stress when He does!

LEAÐIṄG iṅ tHE SPiRit

While in the act of leading worship, spiritual discernment is also needed. Your plan may be carefully honed and spiritually guided, but its execution is still in need of the Spirit's guidance. Remember your motive is always to shepherd the people and to meet their needs. Always ask the Lord to check your motives, that they would be pure and in your people's best interests. Maintain the congregation, as explained in the last section.

On a practical level, it seems wise to have some predetermined forks in the road. Follow the forks depending on the responses or the need of the moment. Such forks could be, "We will sing this chorus through, either two times or three, depending on how people are responding. And then, we will either do a quiet repeating tag (which we practice in advance), or we will keep in tempo and segue immediately into the new song (which we *also* practice in advance)."

The Spirit has already planned some wonderful things for your congregation; don't squelch it by being rigidly tied to your plans. Do not put out the Spirit's fire (1 Thess. 5:19). Do not rely on music to substitute for the Spirit. Do not simply choose songs from your "hot list," or brainstorm on a theme, or develop a song set, and then think that worship leading is merely carrying out the plan for the congregation. Instead, personally hunger for and seek the Lord on a daily basis. We cannot take people where we are not willing to go ourselves. On Sundays, our job is to sense the needs and responses in the people, and to listen to the Spirit's gentle promptings. It's not all about a song list; it's all about God being among His people!

SERVING FRESH BREAD

God demonstrated provision for the children of Israel by giving them manna every day in the wilderness. The manna came each day without fail. For the security freaks, who wanted to save ahead for a rainy day, there was no way to collect more than one day's supply. And for the lazyheads, who didn't collect a full daily supply, God still supplied exactly what was needed. So there was no want among them (*see* Exod. 16:16-20; 2 Cor. 8:13-15).

When we come to God's Word to collect for our daily needs of wisdom and strength (watching daily at wisdom's door; Proverbs 8:34), we can claim this as a not-too-far-fetched promise: God gives us exactly what we need for today, no more and no less. He is always on time, never early and never late. And He is always sufficient.

Worship leaders likewise need to come with fresh bread to the assembly every time. Manna is one of the spiritual lessons from the children of Israel in the desert that God intends for us today. They could not live on yesterday's manna; it rotted. They could not gather for tomorrow's meals. Every day they were dependent on the Lord to supply miraculously for their daily needs. We must bring fresh bread, not stale or reheated. Go to the well, watch daily at the doors of wisdom, devote yourself to the ministry of the Word and prayer, and come to Jesus, the Bread of Life.

Let's add more biblical stories to this point: a boy gave all that he had one day, five loaves and two fish, and a multitude was fed (*see* John 6:9). Would the crowd have experienced the miracle if the boy had given up only two loaves and one fish? I don't know, but the point is that he gave all he had to eat, with no idea where more would come from. Jesus said to give no thought for tomorrow, what you will eat, or what you will wear, but that each day has enough trouble of its own (Matt. 6:25-34).

So, as worship planners and worship leaders, we need to never hold back our best, afraid that we will not be able to "top" this week's assembly if we give our all. Let's give to the Lord with sweet abandon, use it all up, pour it all out, and allow our heavenly Father to give us this day our daily bread.

Trying to give fresh bread does not mean we must be original all the time! Use the best ideas, songs, prayers, and plans you find from others.[44] Certainly there are also time constraints on our planning, or skill limitations in the leader, where we must rely on a prepackaged meal, rather than cooking from scratch. But the concept of fresh bread is that we will prayerfully tailor our plan to meet the needs of our local church this week. Even when reusing songs or sets, try to add a new spark of creativity, bathed in prayer, to meet the needs of the moment, not of last week or last year or the last church you served.

WHAT IF . . .

If the Lord were to remove His Holy Spirit from the church, I wonder how long it would be before anyone noticed? This is totally hypothetical, because we have the promise that God would not do so (John 14:16), but if the Spirit *were* removed, what would be different?

I'd *like* to think that it would go like this for me: In my planning, I would be very distressed; the song list would not be coming together, I'd feel out of sorts, abandoned, and empty; that I'd have no idea how to proceed. I could create a song list that "works," in that the keys, the themes, and the tempos all work together, but something wasn't right about it. Then, I'd like to think that I would arrive for practice with the worship team, and say, "I don't know what's wrong; I have heard nothing from the Lord. I need your help." I'd like to think that they would get on their knees and pray, desperate to know what was wrong; and finding no solution, that we would all come before the congregation empty, and have no music. I'd like to imagine that the congregation would be out of sorts, hopeless and powerless, and surprised that they had come and just hadn't "gotten through" with their prayers and their other acts of worship.

What I *fear*, though, is that all would go as usual in most of our churches. The songs would be chosen based on how they fit the theme and how well they flowed together musically. The musicians would rehearse and learn their music just like normal. The congregation would experience the same thing they always experience—a fine, well-organized service with a good teaching from the Bible, and comfortable routines. Sunday morning and all's well. Worship planning, worship leading, and worship in the soul.[45]

What a terrible, condemning thought, that we would not even notice if the Spirit were missing! Or that we have a hard time in this hypothetical example even imagining what we, in fact, rely on the Spirit to do! May we repent of doing in the flesh what should only be done in the Spirit.

A Final Word

Every sermon is worship, and adds to the collection. Every devotional reading time, every prayer, every deed done in the name of Jesus is another step in the journey of our worship pilgrimage. To borrow from John, Jesus alone is worthy of every word in every book, which might fill the whole world if they were written.

Life is a journey, and worship practices change constantly. What I hope to have contributed is a book that can serve as a practical resource through the changes of style and repertoire and still serve as a practical compass for you. You may find some necessary elements are missing. You may find yourself strongly disagreeing with some of the things presented. Even so, may you enjoy the journey of discovering God's best for you.

The peace of Christ be with you.

Reflection/Application

This project would work best with a group of three or four people. Set aside about an hour for this project: Brainstorm and craft an assembly, assuming that the message would be based on the text of John 3:16.

1. First, appoint one person to be the "preacher" in your group, and have him or her choose the part(s) of the verse that will be emphasized in the message (e.g., grace, God's love, Jesus' death, etc.). This should take about 1 minute.

2. Then, brainstorm a list of about 30 songs. Be sure that some of the songs are calls to worship or general praise songs, some fit in with the theme, and some are more worship or consecration songs. Be sure to keep balance with hymns, gospel songs, classic choruses and newer choruses. This stage should take about 15 minutes.

3. Now brainstorm on some presentation songs, drama sketches, related Scriptures to read, video clips to show, and other creative items to help focus the theme. Write it all down on a large piece of paper. This may take another 15 minutes.

4. Next, assign one person in the group to narrow the choices by selecting about eight songs and one or two of the creative elements, and to put them into a tentative order. This could be done separately, or in front of the rest of the group. It should take about 10 minutes.

5. Walk through the tentative assembly events, and have the group refine the plan in another brainstorm. This should take about 15 minutes.

6. Write down your "final" order of service.

ПOTES

PREFACE

[1] These especially tended to be the more affluent downtown churches, which added organs, accepted missionary societies, and leaned toward liberalism and the social gospel.

[2] They resisted the addition of musical instruments, emphasized evangelism and local congregational autonomy, and had a stricter view of scriptural authority in their theology.

CHAPTER TWO

[1] Lesson/Proclamation and Evangelism were not on Alexander Campbell's list of five essentials that are nonnegotiable New Testament acts of the assembly.

CHAPTER THREE

[1] Tommy Tenney, *The God Chasers* (Shippensburg, PA: Destiny Image Publishers, 1998), pp. 54-55.

[2] *Worship Songs of the Vineyard*, Songbook, Volume 7, published in the late 1990s. Significantly, Vineyard's main publishing arm is called Mercy Music, or Mercy/Vineyard Publishing.

[3] *The New Strong's Exhaustive Concordance of the Bible.*

[4] Check out Clinton Pratt's musical setting for this gem at www.cbyondmusic.org. Downloads are free!

[5] "One Day" words by J. Wilbur Chapman (1859-1918).

[6] "Lord, I Lift Your Name on High" by Rick Founds. Copyright 1989 by Maranatha! Music. All rights reserved.

[7] Within the last century, there have been different manifestations of The Presence among experientialists (see chapter 4). Some sing and pray, asking God to send His power as He had at Pentecost. They might work themselves into a frenzied state, and the manifestations begin. Others sense a mysterious Presence, felt but not seen. They might gather and experience a manifestation during group open worship or during prayer and ministry times. Still others set the mood with music, and The Presence is felt and gifts released. Yet others are open to "something," but often taken by surprise. The manifestation might be independent of music or any other setting.

[8] The tabernacle was God's specific plan. He was pleased with it, because *He visited it with His presence*; a pillar of cloud by day and of fire by night showed that God chose to dwell there. The temple seems to have been David's idea, but God *visited it with His presence*; at the dedication, smoke filled the temple. The synagogue was not initiated by God's specific biblical command, yet, He chose to *visit it with His presence* in the person of Jesus, who made it His regular practice to attend the synagogue. The church was God's plan from ages past, and *He visited it with His presence* when His Spirit manifested itself with tongues of flame, and then through signs and wonders. Even today, the scattered, imperfect, unauthorized, persecuted church, sometimes without clergy and without a building, is blessed by God's presence.

[9] Chuck Fromm points out that to the early church the presence was found in the Eucharist, the Reformers shifted it to the Word, and this generation finds it in music.

[10] "Is it pleasing to people" would not fairly represent the anthropocentric view. Meeting needs is a significantly different motivation than pleasing people.

[11] The liturgy of the Word, the part of the assembly that was designed for visitors.

CHAPTER FOUR

[1] Here are the two solutions:

[2] The movement was introduced in the Foreword of this book.

[3] Ironically, the centrist Restoration churches have no music publisher of their own, and so purchase virtually all of their materials for congregational singing from outside sources.

[4] Take the matter of church polity as an example. USAmerican churches value local autono-

my and individual freedom. Churches are independent, ignoring the apostolic authority and inter-dependence of early churches. (Can you imagine Timothy sending a resume and sample sermon to Ephesus to apply for the pulpit ministry there?) Many churches still tend to make decisions and elect leadership by secret ballot, which seems more based on American democracy than on biblical precedent. Congregational "business meetings" are a concept borrowed from American business, not the Scriptures. And in recent years, most ministers have been more influenced by leadership and management principles learned from American business than from study and prayer. Church buildings themselves are built for comfort, and "successful" churches are growing numerically, which is the American way.

[5]In all fairness, we should also watch against favoritism in the other direction, as well. For some, it is easier to minister to people who are at or below their socio-economic level. In truth, some of us are more comfortable talking to people who don't intimidate us with their education or their wealth. Any selfish profiling is not right, even if it appears to be noble profiling.

[6]Chapter 53 of the Rule begins: "Let all guests who arrive be received as Christ, because He will say:'I was a stranger and you took Me in' (Matt. 25:35)." The *Holy Rule* is often cited for ush-ering in a long-standing tradition of "Benedictine hospitality" to guests. Special care is to be shown in receiving "poor people and pilgrims, because in them more particularly Christ is received" (*RB* 53:15). The monks are to meet guests "with all the courtesy of love" (53:3). A visiting monk is to "be received for as long a time as he wishes," and even his criticisms, if reasonable, are to be heed-ed carefully as possible messages from the Lord (61:3-4). The porter is always to be available to visitors with a spirit of gratitude for their presence and is to speak to them "with the warmth of love" (66:2-4).

[7]Notice the phrases drawn from this chapter: **"But everyone who prophesies speaks to men for their strengthening, encouragement and comfort"** (v. 3). **"He who prophesies edifies the church"** (v. 4). **"He who prophesies is greater than the one who speaks in tongues [because] the church may be edified"** (v. 5). **"Since you are eager to have spiritual gifts, try to excel in gifts that build up the church"** (v. 12). **"[If you are speaking in tongues] you may be giving thanks well enough, but the other man is not edified"** (v. 17). **"All of these [psalm, instruction, revelation, tongue, or interpretation] must be done for the strengthening of the church"** (v. 26). **"For you can all prophesy in turn so that everyone may be instructed and encouraged"** (v. 31).

[8]Perhaps this twofold concept is what Jesus meant by worship "in spirit and in truth" (John 4:24), or the psalmist when he wrote, **"May the words of my mouth and the meditation of my heart be pleasing in your sight, O Lord, my Rock and my Redeemer"** (Ps. 19:14).

[9]Now, some clarification:"Amen" means,"So be it," or "May it come to be." It does *not* mean, "I agree with your opinion." If I say,"The world is going to hell in a hand basket, and Christians are just sitting on their hands letting it happen!" you might agree with me, but saying,"Amen" would not be appropriate. You can say,"yes," or "you're right," or "I agree," but don't say,"amen," because you don't *want* it to happen! When Jesus said,"Verily, verily I say unto you," (KJV) or "Truly, truly . . . " (NAS) or "I tell you the truth" (NIV), each time those phrases come up, the Greek words of Jesus are,"Amen, Amen."

[10]Something similar also happened to Jesus, as recorded in John 7:45-49, when soldiers who were sent to capture Jesus returned empty handed, saying,"No one ever spoke like this before!" Paul may have also been thinking of Numbers 11:29, where Moses wished "that all the Lord's peo-ple were prophets and that the Lord would put his Spirit on them!"

[11]Elisha asked for a harpist to be brought to him, and **"while the harpist was playing, the hand of the Lord came upon Elisha"** and he prophesied (2 Kings 3:15). Even backslidden Saul was given to occasional prophecy while David played his harp (1 Samuel 18:10). Phrases are often linked togeth-er in Scripture, such as **"Sing to him, sing praise to him; tell of all his wonderful acts"** (1 Chronicles 16:9). Many prophetic oracles are written in poetic form, such as the books of Nahum and Habakkuk; also, Lamentations, Joel, Amos, Obadiah, Micah and Zephaniah contain a prophetic message from the Lord, and are poems. In 1 Chronicles 25:1, David sets apart some of the sons of Asaph, Heman and Jeduthun **"for the ministry of prophesying, accompanied by harps, lyres and cymbals."**

[12]Check out Acts 13:1-5. The church in Antioch had five prophets and teachers functioning. How do you think they did that, practically?

[13]Most churches don't need to worry a lot about this. We've got the decency-and-in-order thing down pretty well. We don't have everybody trying to share while the preacher is talking.

[14]We have a web page on the CByond site dedicated to what we call "Ancient Evangelical Worship." You may want to visit it: www.cbyondmusic.org/orthodox_worship/ancient.html.

[15]For example, "liturgy" only serves as a noun, not a verb or an adjective. You don't say, "I'm going to liturgy God now," or "That's a great liturgy song."

[16]See chapter 5 for a more extensive treatment of Scripture reading in the assembly.

[17]Ronald Allen and Gordon Borror, *Worship: Rediscovering the Missing Jewel* (Portland, OR: Multnomah Press, 1982).

[18]The Pentecostal movement sprang from the Holiness/Wesleyan tradition, starting in 1906 with the Azusa Street church (and shortly thereafter from several other churches around the country). Some denominations of Pentecostal churches are Apostolic, Church of God (Cleveland, TN), Church of God in Christ, United Pentecostal Church, Church of the Foursquare Gospel, and Assemblies of God.

[19]This was related to the Latter Rain movement, which tied the outpouring of the Spirit with sure signs of the soon coming of Christ.

[20]Besides The Vineyard, some charismatic groups are Christ's Church Fellowship, Calvary Chapel, and many independent churches.

[21]Such churches as Brownsville Assembly of God and Toronto Airport Church and many others report spontaneous revival outbreaks that last for weeks, months, or years.

[22]The sign gifts tend to center around tongues (especially), interpretation, healing, prophetic utterances, and other so-called manifestation gifts of the Spirit.

[23]Mostly-charismatic publishing houses are Maranatha! Music, Vineyard/Mercy Music, Integrity Music and most of the other publishers that specialize in choruses.

[24]Slaves in the South were especially in a hopeless situation; families were broken apart, difficult or cruel slave owners owned and could legally abuse people through their entire lives. There was no hope of escape, except after this life. So when black slaves gathered, sometimes in secret, those who were believers "sought renewal, restoration and reaffirmation of the control of Almighty God in their disrupted and confused lives."

[25]This trend seems to be changing among many young GenX church planters, I'm happy to say.

[26]The blend shows in music, and also in political and sociological matters crossing over into the church.

[27]My apologies to John Piper. He has wonderful insights and uses this term to make a valid point.

[28]Note that in the Old Testament, the only time that God manifested His presence and clarified His blessings in a daily, tangible way, it turned out to be an abysmal failure. That was the Exodus Experiment. The people grumbled almost from the first day, and when God called them to step out in faith and enter the Promised Land, after having miraculously cared for them, they saw the people as giants and voted 3 million-to-2 (or 3, if you count the vote of Moses) against obeying the Lord.

[29]The most common term for worship in the New Testament epistles is *latreuo*, which has to do with indirect priestly service to God, rather than bowing before a physical presence.

[30]What used to be called "special music" in many churches, it is music that is performed with the intent that others will listen, rather than participate. Choir anthems, solos with trax, video clips, and sermons all fall under the category of "presentational."

[31]Read Revelation 3:15-22.

[32]Compare 2 Timothy 4:3 and 3:4,5 with 1 Corinthians 14:24,25.

CHAPTER FIVE

[1]Hippolytus wrote this as a report of the prayer he remembers hearing in his boyhood, therefore, this prayer probably dates to A.D. 150.

[2]In a sense, a sermon as such is not necessary; Alexander Campbell did not include it in his list of nonnegotiables, and the church service that he described used sharing by various members toward the edification of the Body, rather than a central sermon.

[3]The emphasis is not that the act of preaching is foolish, but that the message is foolish. Either way, preaching is the essential vehicle.

[4]This was addressed earlier. *See* Chapter 4.

[5]Some traditions call this "witnessing." ("Can I have a witness?") After the message, elders and members concur, illustrate, or perhaps disagree with the teaching from the sermon.

[6]I am choosing not to address the issue of worship practice or style of music here. My concern is with text only.

[7]André Resner, Jr., "Lament: Faith's Response to Loss," *Restoration Quarterly*, 32/3 (1990): 129-142.

[8]Resner, "Lament,: p. 132.

[9]See summary chart on p. 26 of *Person and Number* (see fn 10 below).

[10]The standard of the Psalms has been further documented in the author's thesis, *An Analysis of Person and Number in Selected Hymnals in Light of the Psalms*, unpublished master's thesis (Cincinnati, OH: Cincinnati Bible College & Seminary, 1986), pp. 2-4.

[11]Artur Weiser, *The Psalms* (Philadelphia: Westminster Press, 1962), pp. 52ff.

[12]This difference is reflected in the average of only 1.3 topics per chorus against almost 1.9 topics per psalm.

CHAPTER SIX

[1]"How to Reach the Baby Boomer: Ministering to the 21st-Century Church," 1990 seminar by Elmer Towns.

[2]Towns says that whatever music you listened to between the ages of 10 and 13 will always be your "heart music."

[3]Leviticus 19:32 commands the Israelites to stand in the presence of the aged and to respect older people.

[4]Here is an irony of history: A slogan in the '60s was, "never trust anyone over 30." Now that all Boomers are older than 30, I wonder how they feel about that watchword?

[5]However, they are rapidly losing their influence, and are being pushed out by the next generation, starting with the Internet, music, technology, and entertainment industries.

[6]These worldview concepts are drawn from "The Emerging Culture," an article by Paul H. Ray published in *American Demographics*, Feb. 1997.

[7]My gratitude to Andrew Greeley for his insights in his chapter on the liturgy of the future in his 1969 book *Religion in the Year 2000* (New York: Sheed and Ward, 1969), which often overlap what I have written here.

[8]So, is it "right" for worship to be mystically sexual with the Lord? Let's quickly examine the reasoning. 1) We are commanded to love God with all of our heart, soul, mind, and strength, and we are to present our bodies to Him as living sacrifices. Yet that love is *agape* love, not *eros*. And we are also to love our neighbor as we love ourselves, but that is not by any means intended to be sexually demonstrated! 2) Paul said that his desire was to know Christ, and he used the same word as is used in Genesis for Adam knowing his wife. But that knowing is not yet fulfilled, as I Corinthians 13 says: *Then* we will know fully, even as we are known. 3) If we are the Bride of Christ, should we not be intimate with our groom? That depends on whether or not the wedding has taken place! Christ considers us His bride, but He is waiting to present us to Himself as a spotless Bride at the great wedding feast. Until then, the whole point of the bride analogy is that we are keeping ourselves pure as we *wait* for consummation. 4) The common New Testament word

for worship is *proskuneo,* which means "to kiss the hand toward." But what is the image drawn in that term? It is of bowing before and kissing the ring of the king, or of kneeling before the subject's lord. That is by no means "kissing God" or being intimate with Him. It is precious, it is sacred, but it is not sexual! 5) What about Song of Solomon? Depending on how you interpret that book, it could be about the relationship of Christ to His church. If so, there is very much sexual allegory there. And the German pietists (Neander, Zinzendorf) often wrote hymns of love from bride to Christ. One music minister several years ago wrote in his church's newsletter, *[Worship] is simply what lovers do. They caress, they extol each other's beauty, they weep with longing, they plumb the depths of intimate knowledge. This, turned to song, becomes the psalm of the bride's desire for her bridegroom, of the soul's yearning for its redeemer. It is the music of the intimate place, the melody of shared presence. This is what the hungry heart seeks.* Are we one with Christ, or are we still *longing* to be one with Him? 6) It is not new to somehow involve sexual acts in worship. Much pagan worship of the past, and even today, involves temple prostitutes and deviant behavior. Certainly such behavior is not what our Lord desires.

[9]A 1995 chorus entitled "You Are My Passion" refers to Jesus as "my Lover" and speaks of longing for his touch, waiting to be gathered in His arms, and hearing His beating heart ("You Are My Passion," by Noel and Tricia Richards. © 1995 Kingsway's Thankyou Music). We can use the word picture to realize that we are talking about spiritual things in physical terms. Recently, a worship leader, in the height of worship time, called out "Let's make love to Jesus!"

[10]U2 is a secular/worship crossover band, and John Denver's "You Fill Up My Senses" would be a popular worship song, given the right introduction. The Beatles' "Come Together," with a few changes, has made a powerful worship song.

[11]Andrew Greeley, *Religion in the Year 2000,* pp. 134-136. "The major development [in the future] will be a dramatic resurgence of the Dionysian in the liturgy, the first signs of which, one supposes, are the guitars and the stomping feet of the Roman Catholic folk liturgy. Liturgy will then be used quite consciously to promote the release of non-rational and ecstatic forces in man—to take him out of himself, to open people up to one another, and to enrich and reinforce community ties in which a man finds himself. Liturgy will then turn to the popular arts . . . and particularly to those forms of popular art which seem most ecstatic. It will become quite self-conscious about its own Dionysian character and very explicit about its own therapeutic intent. . . . the use of liturgy to create community, or at least to reinforce it, is likely to increase. . . . Theologizing about the dignity and the fulfillment of the human personality will also lead, one suspects, to an increased liturgical emphasis on self-fulfillment, self-development, and self-expression in liturgy which may come to mean that eventually everyone will have to play the guitar."

[12]These churches are those who conclude that the assembly for them is primarily for worship.

[13]Of course, these churches conclude that the assembly is primarily for evangelism.

[14]Actually, this is a grave concern to me. The church today has many parallels to the evangelicals of a century ago. Back then, the Salvation Army and the YMCA were models of both evangelical zeal and of social justice. The first generation built such organizations on a strong Bible basis. But future generations were not trained in the biblical "why" for social programs. So, they subtly changed the organizations into nonoffensive humanitarian efforts, aimed at making life on earth better for people, without demonstrating a concern for eternity. The social gospel movement today is but a shadow of its former self. Likewise, today's evangelicals are rediscovering the need for social justice and for acts of kindness, but they are not all learning the biblical foundations for such theology. They begin their mode of evangelism and preaching with anthropology, rather than theology. Therefore, without a major change, the next generation will do goodwill on earth, but will not prepare people well for heaven.

[15]Many churches are starting midweek celebration services, which are contemporary in style. Since they are not "sacramental," they are not as divisive as a new Lord's Day assembly might be. But they could speak the heart language of many of the people who are not as reached on the first day of the week.

[16]Michael S. Hamilton, "The Triumph of the Praise Songs," *Christianity Today,* July 12, 1999, p. 30.

¹⁷Of course, if the assembly is for outreach, then the needs of targeted groups of people supersede the needs of the family.

¹⁸They may genuinely think that they represent the majority. But experience seems to indicate that they really only know their own circle of friends.

¹⁹For example, the other day at a multichurch gathering of people with mostly white hair, I was surprised to hear how strongly they sang out on the chorus of "Shout to the Lord."

²⁰Can you have cheap aesthetics? Most evangelical churches would not even consider commissioning major works of art to display in the building.

²¹Proverbs counsels us not to hire *"a fool, or any passer-by"* (Prov. 26:10).

Chapter Seven

¹Of course, I mean no disrespect to other staff positions. This may not be accurate, and it is impossible to compare necessary skills. But if you could disregard whatever offense might be aroused and follow the train of thought in this chapter, you will see that it is a daunting task. Robert Webber says, "Preparation for worship leadership is more comprehensive in nature and scope than anything else in ministry."

²Did you ever wonder how our Lord would have done as a preacher in a local church?

³A growing number are open to having a woman in this role, but it is still rather rare in the Bible Belt.

⁴*See* Jeremiah 23:1-4 and Ezekiel 34:2-24 for what is largely the opposite of the role of a shepherd. See also John 21:15-17.

⁵The connection of prophecy and music was further discussed back in chapter 4.

⁶A sacrament is a mystery in which the presence of Christ is found.

⁷The Spirit bearing witness with our spirit that we are the sons of God — Romans 8:16.

⁸Bill Gothard uses this model.

⁹Thanks to Dr. Harold Best for this insight.

¹⁰This list comes to me from the teaching of John G. Elliott.

¹¹Again, this is John Elliott's list, and is in contrast to the previous one.

¹²On the day of Pentecost, the disciples were ridiculed after receiving the baptism of the Holy Spirit by being called drunk on new wine (how appropriate was the terminology!) (Acts 2:13) Later, Paul says not to be drunk with wine, but to be filled with the Spirit. (Eph. 5:18)

Chapter Eight

¹You know, freedom isn't free if there are places you can't go. So if you can't borrow from the liturgy, or if you can't do something sensitive to seekers, your worship is defined by what you *don't* do, rather than by what you do.

²Which includes all of those assessments from chapters one and two.

³Songs, transitions, medleys, sketches, video clips, prayers, readings, testimonies, and other activities.

⁴Here I contrast two types of planning: event orientation, in which the order of worship centers around the events (prayer hymn, prayer, communion hymn, meditation, prayer, etc.); and worship set orientation, in which the order centers around the sense of flow of emotion or how the theme best unfolds.

⁵The Praise set consists of opening songs, inviting people to join in general exaltation. The Theme set advances the central message of the day, and may contain the focus statement and/or lead into the message. The Worship set might be centered around the Lord's Supper, or perhaps around an extended prayer time.

⁶Inviting people to worship, engaging in active praise, and then focusing down into more intimate adoration.

⁷This fourfold pattern highlights the structure of liturgical churches, and is advocated by

Robert Webber and others. Remember, it is only an order for structuring your events, not a style or a theology.

[8]In many RM churches, communion is placed ahead of the sermon. We express worship, then respond with Table. Then we hear the Word and respond with Invitation to Discipleship.

[9]This way of planning would work for many traditional RM churches. Sing two or three songs of praise, and then plan songs around the Table. The rest of the service is determined by the series of events.

[10]Most often, the worship set would be in the place of opening praise. Then the rest of the service consists of prayer, communion, offering, special music, Scripture reading, sermon, invitation, and closing.

[11]This authority is important to clarify, or there can be sudden confusion or anarchy on a Sunday morning. One member of the team might anticipate slowing down, another thinks we should repeat the song one more time, and another wants to go on to the next song. If they all agree to follow the designated leader at those times, the confusion is resolved.

[12]Notice this is not necessarily "old" and "new." Hymns are unfamiliar to those who have never been to church, for example.

[13]An example of an exception would be the beginning of a conference, where you can introduce several new songs in the first meeting, but use them all week long, and aim for the peak of freshness to be the last session.

[14]Some of those musical elements are: change the instruments, the tempo, the "groove," the key or voicing, remove all instruments, add a modulation, set it to a different tune, use only the chorus, etc. This is why the worship leader needs to be a creative arranger, as was mentioned in chapter 7.

[15]You can read a Scripture to shed new light on it, tell a hymn story or other background for it, have someone share a testimony or other insight that will emphasize a particular truth in the song's text, teach some doctrinal truth that is highlighted in the song, etc.

[16]Play a CD of the song during prelude, have the choir sing it as a "special" the week before you introduce it to the congregation, or use the solo verse/chorus format and invite the congregation to sing along on the last time through the chorus, as examples.

[17]As examples: project the words or provide printed music, explain what part the men and women sing ahead of time, make the melody clear in your sound mix, and more.

[18]While often a song needs a "frame" of silence in order to sink in, other times the pause is awkward and breaks the concentration of the worshiper as the leader moves his capo. The rule of thumb is that people should wait on the Lord, but should never wait on you. If they don't need silence, find a way to segue from one song to the next.

[19]See elsewhere in this chapter, where the concept of mechanics is explained.

[20]Some song leaders use only this filter when ordering their songs, making worship leading mere emotional manipulation. While that is a serious problem, levels of emotion should, in fact, be given serious consideration. It is one of the filters, not the only filter.

[21]Other patterns are also effective. For example, many churches start with quiet reflection and work their way slowly up to celebration.

[22]Exhortation songs would say things like, "Come and worship the Lord," or "We will enter His gates and sing His praise," or "Sing to God, all you saints," or "You are a chosen generation."

[23]Prayer songs have phrases like, "I love You, Lord," or "You are good to me," or "Great are Your works, O Lord," or "Jesus, You are my Treasure."

[24]I recognize that the Psalms themselves occasionally shift back and forth from exhortation to prayer and back again. So this principle is not an absolute. But try to be sensitive to the discerning worshipers, and let them stay in prayer once they get there.

[25]Some churches teach that corporate expressions of worship are the only proper ones. Indeed, in the New Testament, Christ hymns tend to be collective, objective, doctrinal declarations of

Christ. But many of the Psalms are very personal, and it is certainly right to give personal expressions in public.

²⁶Some have likened this pattern to the tabernacle. We enter His gates and into His courts with celebration and as a group. But we eventually find our way to the Holy of Holies, and we must go there alone.

²⁷In my experience and my opinion, many worship programming teams fall into a fault when they start brainstorming around a theme. The theme becomes more important than the connection with God. You want to craft inductive worship, not deductive lessons. Only rarely will four-point lessons work in guiding genuine worship.

²⁸Aiming for too many "moments" in one service can seem contrived and emotionally manipulative, and it causes people to not trust you the next time you try to take them deep.

²⁹This kind of flexibility and discernment calls for spiritual sensitivity and musical skill on the part of the leader, and trust of the leader on the part of the worship team.

³⁰I define hymns as those great texts of history, generally doctrinally rich, with dense texts, majestic tunes, and straight rhythms.

³¹Gospel songs started in the mid-nineteenth century and are still written today. They include evangelistic songs of personal testimony with a lilting rhythm and sweeping melody. The tradition continues through songs of Bill Gaither and Andre Crouch, and on to Brooklyn Tabernacle songs, gospel quartet music and Black gospel songs of today.

³²"Classic" choruses are those from the 1960s–1980s, which have found their way into the common repertoire of the church at large.

³³Hymns, gospel songs, and many "classic" choruses are generally keyboard-driven, but most of the recent choruses and songs are very much guitar-driven. The newer choruses may become "classic" someday. No doubt songs like "Shout to the Lord" and "Open the Eyes of My Heart" are well on their way to "classic" status already.

³⁴The theme could also follow the church year (Advent, Christmas, Easter, Pentecost, etc.), or some other outside influence, rather than the spoken message (such as a revival or guest speaker or worship leader). Sometimes, the preacher cannot give the topic enough in advance to do much planning. Other times, some circumstance makes it impractical to build around the message (such as a tragedy within the church).

³⁵It could end with quiet personal prayer, or a public call to repentance, or a standard invitation, or perhaps an exciting response to the Good News.

³⁶Well, okay, the topic of adultery might be a bit of a challenge. When you look in the topical index of your hymnal for "Adultery," you won't find many hymns. But you could turn even a tough topic like this one into worship by singing about God's faithfulness, or exploring His holiness, or singing about our need for mercy, or by upholding marriage as honorable before God. Any worthy topic can become a worship topic, if given a holy spin.

³⁷Take the doctrine of Salvation by Grace as an example: Those who are in Christ have been saved by grace. Now, say it back to God: "Lord, you have redeemed us. I am alive because of Your grace to me. You are loving in all that You do, and faithful to me. I praise You."

³⁸I slipped once and said, "Be sure to worship yourself." But that's not quite the message I wanted to convey. ☺

³⁹I made a mistake when I planned to move communion to the end of a service in order to highlight it. I thought I had done all of my groundwork well. The preacher agreed, the elders agreed, the servers were notified, and the plan was ready. But I hadn't thought of the children's workers. The servers were in the practice of serving the congregation, then two of them went out the back doors and served the children's workers. The workers planned their lessons around this, with an interruption usually coming about halfway through the hour. When the server came to the door, it was while workers were wrapping up lessons, putting away materials, and getting ready for parents to come. That was a good idea that worked in the worship center, but not elsewhere in the building!

[40] The surest way to drive away a musician is to continually expect too much, without enough preparation time. Your pianist and organist are among your greatest assets. Be sure to keep them happy!

[41] I know the statement, "It's better to ask forgiveness than to ask for permission." But you protect yourself if you have everything cleared with the elders and the preacher (who is your supervisor, even if the by-laws don't say so). If they approved, they can defend you when (note: not *if*) people complain about something.

[42] They might get this worship participation philosophy from 1 Corinthians 14:26, assuming that each person comes with a psalm.

[43] In many congregations, for example, they stand and sing the "Doxology" at the end of the offering. Everyone in the congregation knows it is coming, but it is an embarrassing surprise to the uninitiated.

[44] In fact, learning and borrowing from others is the major point of chapters three and four.

[45] If a "secret rapture" of the saints were to occur at midnight on a Saturday, how full would our churches be the next morning?

About the Author

Ken Read approaches the subject of leading Christian worship both as a teacher and a practitioner, serving as Professor of Music and Worship at Cincinnati Bible College and Seminary and as a servant shepherd at Community Christian Church of Northern Kentucky. He earned a 1980 BM in Music Theory at the University of Cincinnati, then received his MM in 1992 from Miami University in Theory/Composition. He has two degrees from Cincinnati Bible Seminary, an MA in Practical Theology (1986) and the MMin in Church Music (1993). His doctorate was the DMA from University of Kentucky School of Fine Arts, awarded in 1995 in the field of Composition.

He has held ministries in music and worship in Ohio, Illinois, and Kentucky, including two church plants. In addition to his responsibilities with the College/Seminary and his present ministry, he serves on the Executive Committee of the National Church Music Conference.

Ken has been married to Ellen, his high school youth group sweetheart, for 21 years as of the publication of this book. The couple have 6 children, and base their ministry around hospitality.

As you have insights and suggestions, you are cordially invited to share them with the author at: ken.read@cincybible.edu .

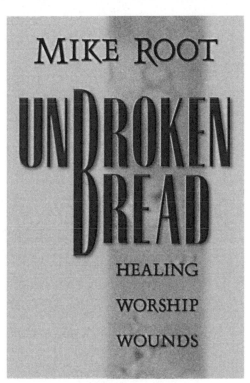